Economic Development in the Digital Age

Nagy K. Hanna

Economic Development in the Digital Age

palgrave
macmillan

Nagy K. Hanna
Bethesda, MD, USA

ISBN 978-3-031-54568-9   ISBN 978-3-031-54569-6 (eBook)
https://doi.org/10.1007/978-3-031-54569-6

This Palgrave Macmillan imprint is published by the registered company Springer Nature Switzerland AG
The registered company address is: Gewerbestrasse 11, 6330 Cham, Switzerland

Paper in this product is recyclable.

Acknowledgments

I am indebted to Anil Srivastava for inspiring me to write this memoir. Also thanks to Kiran Karnik for writing the preface.

I am grateful to Asya Rudkovskaya for her role as lead editor and thoughtful commentator.

My advocacy meeting with Kristalina Georgieva, then the CEO of the World Bank, was brief but influenced her decision to elevate the digital development function at the World Bank. Thanks to Jim Wolfensohn, then Bank President, Mohamed Muhsin, then CIO, and Praful Patel, then regional VP, who gave me the opportunity to collaborate with Sri Lankan policy makers on a pioneering digital transformation project.

I am grateful to Shinji Asanuma, Robert Picciotto, and Paul Isenman, as they generously shared their insights. Thanks to colleagues who influenced my thinking and commented on my drafts: Luci Abrahams, Klaus Tilmes, Tim Kelly, Peter Knight, Carlo Rossotto, Samia Melhem, Eduardo Talero, and Nigel Cameron. Also grateful to all who gave me their endorsements.

My learning journey through economic development in general and digital development assistance in particular has been shaped by many colleagues at the World Bank, policy makers in developing countries, and academics at universities and think tanks.

Among World Bank leaders and colleagues who influenced my journey, I wish to mention: Mahmoud Mohieldin, Sanjay Pradhan, Peter Harrold, Deepak Mishra, Boutheina Guermazi, Christine Qiang, Philippe Dongier,

Shashank Ojha, Nimrod Raphaeli, Mahfouz Tadros, Ram Agarwala, Khalid Siraj, Dan Ritchie, H. Kohli, Mark Baird, Randeep Sudan, Shaku Gunaratne, Ian Scott, Chuck Zeigler, Helen Vazquez, Peter Scherer, Robert Schware, Carl Dahlman, Oleg Petrov, Carlos Braga, Sandra Sargent, Soniya Carvalho, and Miguel Schloss.

I owe debt to many senior policy makers and development practitioners in developing countries so I only mention those from India and Sri Lanka, the two country case studies: Milinda Moragoda, Eran Wickramaratne, Sam Pitroda, R. Chandrasekhar, Satya Narayanan, F. C. Kohli, K. Roy Paul, Saurabh Srivastava, N. Seshagiri, N. Vittal, Dewang Mehta, Harish Mehta, Lalit Weeratunga, Manju Haththotuwa, Reshan Dewapura, Jayantha Fernando, Wasantha Deshapriya, and Rohan Samarajiva.

Among thought leaders and academics who influenced my thinking I wish to mention: Vint Cerf, Richard Heeks, Robert Wade, Sandor Boyson, Elias Carayannis, Carlota Perez, Ernest Wilson, Dani Rodrik, Albert Hirschman, David Ellerman, Devish Kapur, Mike Porter, and Gunnar Myrdal.

Special thanks to Palgrave's editorial and Springer's production teams for quality work.

Not all of the above agree with my conclusions. I thank them all, without implicating them.

Last but not least, I am indebted to my wife Linda, and son James for bearing my absences while I spent disproportionate time at work and away from home on field missions.

Introduction

The digital revolution is creating unprecedented opportunities and challenges for economic development. Developing countries and aid agencies must embrace digital technologies and reinvent public policies and strategies for digital transformation to tackle interrelated grand development challenges: growing poverty and inequality, hunger and food insecurity, jobs and unemployment, health and pandemics, access to education, governance and corruption, conflicts and security, and water scarcity and climate change. Information and communication technology (ICT) is a general-purpose technology that can be harnessed to provide innovative, powerful, and smart solutions across all these challenges.

This book draws from my long practice in international development assistance driven by a passion to overcome global poverty and fight for justice and inclusion. Throughout the book, I reflect upon my broad experience in strategic planning and development assistance, especially in light of the rise of digitally-enabled development. It is inspired by the revolutionary advances in digital technologies as they offer powerful tools for transforming the development process and shaping the future of humanity. In particular, the recent wave of digital technologies, including artificial intelligence (AI), offers dramatic opportunities and transformational capabilities even while presenting existential risks to societies.

I take a holistic view of digital transformation. I propose an integrated framework that conceives digital transformation as both an *ecosystem* and a *process*. Digital transformation is about using digital technologies to initiate and support deep and sustainable change in structures and processes, modes of production and consumption, value creation from available resources, and/or substantial increases in access to and use of data and knowledge. It is carried out at many levels, including organizations, economic sectors, government functions, cities, and communities. It is also about the restructuring or transforming of whole economies.

Digital transformation is not just about digital connectivity or access to digital technology by individual users. It is about learning to drive digital transformation by the whole society, especially if its full benefits were to be reaped. Access to digital technology must be accompanied by "social software" to secure much of the promised productivity increase and socio-political sustainability. That means building and orchestrating collateral cultural, governance, institutional, and organizational changes.

A digital transformation ecosystem would include enabling policies and regulations, national information and communication infrastructures, data sharing systems, digital sector production and usage competencies, public digital platforms, digital identification infrastructure, digital payment platforms, digital innovation and entrepreneurship ecosystems, and the interactions and partnerships among these foundations. These ecosystem foundations are shared across all digital technologies, including the recent wave of AI-induced transformations. They are crosscutting enablers and building blocks for digital transformation and services at societal scale (World Bank, 2016, 2024; Hanna, 2016).

The book addresses several levels of transformation. A personal transformation journey: from a child distressed by the destitution and human suffering in Cairo's poor neighborhoods into a development practitioner searching for answers to development's key challenges. It draws lessons for development professionals and global aid organizations that must respond to the multiple grand challenges facing humanity today.

The book draws on my personal experience in working with many client countries. It does not represent official positions of the World Bank. Yet, it corroborates and draws on Bank publications and those of other international development agencies. It draws on relatively recent economic growth research that has given due attention to governance, institutions, and leadership (Growth Commission on Growth and Development, 2008; Acemoğlu and Robinson, 2012). These governance issues are often ignored in pursuing digital transformation.

A companion book complements this one and focuses on country case studies and examples of digital transformation at the country, government, city, regional and key economic sector levels. It draws lessons for country policy makers and local stakeholders to guide further digital transformation at all these levels.

Book Organization

First part of the book discusses the broad global economic and technological contexts for development practice and the evolving role of aid agencies, particularly the World Bank. It outlines my motivations to write a book on digital transformation informed by my practice and learning journey. It is about how my experience shaped my tools and frameworks and vice versa. It looks at the lessons I learnt as a development practitioner through the lens of my personal transformation. From projects in Jakarta and Jerusalem to strategic planning at the Bank; from engagements with national governments on designing and implementing digital transformation strategies to advocating digitally-enabled development globally.

My work in the nascent field of digital transformation has taken me through periods of exploration, learning, fulfillment, and growth, but also fear and frustration, bordering on cynicism. It was often difficult to stay focused on addressing urgent client needs in line with my ideals and values while working with weak and often corrupt governments and dealing with the limitations of global aid agencies.

I reflect upon what motivated me to write this book in light of the many challenges facing humanity today: from climate change to growing inequality. I look at the shift in modern development thinking and the evolution of the World Bank. I also share my experiences as I served in various roles and contexts at the Bank and grew my understanding of the actual and potential roles of digital technologies in development. I recall my work in Indonesia and Palestine-Israel that helped me appreciate the demand side of information technologies and drove me to focus on improving the Bank's practice in technical assistance, institutional development, technology and knowledge transfer.

Appointments in the Bank's corporate strategy and performance evaluation functions helped me understand the inner workings of complex aid organizations like the Bank and their rich interactions with country stakeholders. I analyzed best practices to determine how strategic planning should shift from rigid documentation and routine transactions to strategic thinking and agile, adaptive and communication-intensive processes. As a close observer and participant in institutionalizing managerial systems, I came to appreciate the factors influencing the Bank's strategic behavior and limiting aid effectiveness. This informed my search for ways to integrate digital transformation into economic development strategies.

Remaining part of this book discusses the critical barriers to institutional learning and the need for aid organizations to reinvent their services through the use of digital technologies—if they are to keep up with the pace of technological change and stay relevant to their clients.

I trace the Bank's response to the digital revolution starting from the late 1980s, when it was learning to use digital technologies internally while striving to become a knowledge bank. Would the Bank support client countries in rolling out new technologies, building communications infrastructures, and investing in information resources for sustainable development? What factors were influential in recognizing and responding to country needs and demands for digital development assistance? Back then I advocated a proactive approach to apply digital technologies across sectors in Bank-funded development projects. Building ICT assistance competencies would be critical to the Bank's future relevance and the quality of its portfolio across all economic sectors.

Has the World Bank, a premier development agency with over $100 billion in annual lending, lived up to expectations of global leadership in digital development assistance? What factors have determined the success of digital investments in the context of various developing countries? How can aid agencies retool and up their game to help client countries master digital transformation?

I assess formal World Bank corporate strategies for digital transformation practice. Did these strategies address the foundations necessary for building vibrant digital transformation ecosystems? Did they cover strategic applications in key economic sectors? Were they owned by the operating regions within the Bank? Were they seriously followed, monitored, and evaluated? Have aid agencies practice what they preach?

I touch upon several advocacy initiatives I engaged in since leaving the Bank in 2005. I continued to advise Bank colleagues and managers on the future of digital development assistance. I also contributed to the formation of advocacy forums beyond the Bank. These included building digital leadership capacity through creating an e-leadership academy; joining the Wits University of South Africa as visiting professor; contributing to various fora and think tanks; publishing books and articles; and serving on editorial boards. An enduring aim of my post-Bank advisory work remains to advocate for reforming development assistance to address the imperatives of the digital age. This book is an attempt to influence policy makers and practitioners through advocating lessons learnt—the hard way.

In a concluding chapter, I explore the key factors that have delayed the Bank's and other aid agencies' response to today's fast-changing technological environment. I recommend four key elements of a strategy to accelerate institutional learning: strengthening corporate leadership and strategy for digital transformation; mobilizing staff and other resources for the digital future; nurturing a learning and innovation culture; and promoting cross-sector collaboration within and among international aid agencies and country stakeholders.

Praise for *Economic Development in the Digital Age*

"This book, written by prolific author and development intellectual, had my attention from the first page to the last. He has the uncanny ability to see into institutions deeply and to observe digital transformation processes intensely, and to express these insights in ways that enable the reader to see almost as deeply. In this book, Nagy Hanna looks into his own institution, the World Bank and offers analysis of its digital transformation journey, side by side with his own personal journey. He introduces us to brief country narratives from the digital transformation journeys of India, Sri Lanka and Kenya, and a few of the emerging smart city stories: Rio, Singapore, China. If an author were to attempt combining a love story of development practice and a scholarly text on digital transformation, this would be it."

—Luci Abrahams, *Director, LINK Centre, University of the Witwatersrand*

"Digital transformation, as Hanna amply demonstrates, is not just access to digital technology. It is a learning process by the whole society. The stories of Hanna's successes in various countries provide ample insights into digital transformation and its possibilities for development."

—Shinji Asanuma, *Visiting Professor, School of International and Public Policy, Hitotsubashi University*

"As a thought leader, Hanna has accumulated decades of on-the-ground experience pioneering digital transformation projects in economies around the world, the subject of several of his important books. In this culminating and highly-readable volume, he pulls those experiences together, sets them in the context of his life-long career with the Bank, and raises vital questions for every aid agency as we move deeper into the 21st century."

—Nigel Cameron, *President Emeritus, Center for Policy on Emerging Technologies*

"Nagy Hanna shares a lifetime of experience with the deployment of digital technologies in developing countries. Many lessons can be found in this impressive journey."

—Vint Cerf, *Internet pioneer and Hall of Fame member*

"Nagy Hanna exposes the challenges of making technology an effective tool for development, while confronting vested interests that seek to sustain the status quo, both in client governments and internally within the Bank. At the heart of the book is a powerful commitment to learning and using technology to change lives for the better."

—Tim Kelly, *Lead Digital Development Specialist, World Bank*

"As co-author, and fellow digital transformation advocate in and after a career in the World Bank, I heartily endorse Hanna's conclusions. I second his emphasis on 'leadership, shared vision, enabling policies and institutions, upgraded human resources, and national consensus and culture.' Without leadership, it is very difficult to establish holistic digital development policies and get them accepted across siloed sectoral entities, whether within countries or aid agencies."

—Peter T. Knight, *Member, Board of Directors, Fernand Braudel Institute of World Economics*

"What a life! This hugely engaging account of Hanna's career is motivated by his passionate commitment to development and belief in the potential of digital technologies to contribute to inclusive and sustainable development. His acute insights enable him to identify the many risks accompanying digital transformation and the barriers – institutional, political, cultural – to successful outcomes. He calls for holistic approaches to digital development. He emphasizes the crucial need for client buy-in and trust. He insists upon putting multi-stakeholder learning at the core of digital strategies."

—Robin Mansell, *Professor, London School of Economics and Political Science*

"Nagy Hanna has dedicated his career to digital development. He was a pioneer. He created the Bank's digital development community of practice - which mobilized expertise and funding to what was then an innovative new field. Hanna mentored and coached World Bank leadership and staff on technology for development."

—Samia Melhem, *Lead Digital Policy Specialist, World Bank*

"Drawing from his vast experience and pioneering role in the field, Nagy Hanna has woven together a remarkable story of his life and career. The book offers valuable lessons for policy makers and practitioners of digital technology. What Hanna conveys most convincingly is his early insight into the central role of digital technology in development. He illustrates this through examples from his firsthand experience. I had the good fortune to get to know him as a colleague at the World Bank where I witnessed his steadfast pursuit of his pioneering ideas in partnership with the country, and winning over critics. He practiced what he advocates in this book: nurturing local ownership and institutions, co-creating with stakeholders, prioritizing inclusion, and taking a holistic view. This book is a must-read for development professionals."

—Praful Patel, *Former Regional Vice President (Asia), World Bank*

"This book reflects the learning journey of a thought leader and pioneer in harnessing digital technology for development. Through detailed case studies, it ascribes top priority to digital development interventions in diverse country and regional contexts. Hanna's journey combines visionary thinking about digital transformation with hands-on lessons for translating country-driven visions into development programs and projects. He challenges development practitioners, policy makers, aid agencies, and developing countries to re-invent their practices to be fit for the digital age."

—Sam Pitroda, *former advisor to prime ministers of India*

"The author had a distinguished career at the world's most visible international organization. He championed digital transformation and in virtue of his experience, he brings the reader to witness the fascinating evolution of development work across several decades. He describes the tumultuous change brought by technology at a crossroad of geopolitical, cultural and societal changes. In an exercise of retrospect (the author is a passionate art lover), the book reminds us of one of those Flemish paintings where the painter is in the picture, all devoted to providing the proportionate perspective to the external world."

—Carlo Rossotto, *Principal Investment Officer and Global Head, Upstream Telecom Media and Technology Infrastructure, International Finance Corporation*

"Hanna tells an important story of passion and perseverance, as well as doubts and setbacks, with the prize being digital transformation for nations and aid agencies. This book is a timely reminder of what it takes to digitally develop for the benefit of all."

—Jim Spohrer, *Senior executive*

"Nagy Hanna's pioneering study of information technology content of World Bank lending was a wakeup call for Bank leadership. His advocacy for Bank funding the study of India's opportunity for software export led to the exponential growth of India's software sector. I had the privilege of being a participant observer of Hanna's journey as a development economist to a passionate champion of digital transformation. This book shares the trials and triumphs of a developmental practitioner taking up this challenge. The development community needs more of his kind."

—Anil Srivastava, *President, Open Health Systems Lab and Founding Executive Director, NASSCOM*

"Nagy Hanna is one of the foremost digital development pioneers and framers of our time. He had the uncanny ability to see the path ahead, the intellectual curiosity and rigor to refine and apply these insights across a uniquely diverse set of programs and country settings, and the ability to inspire others with his insights about the possibilities of digital transformation to change lives and societies for the better. Hanna's reflections bear testimony of the courage and perseverance required to challenge the status quo, the lifelong passion for learning, and the enduring legacy of having embedded digital innovation into our understanding of development. For multilateral organizations, his book should serve as a wake-up call to re-imagine their mission and ways of doing business in a time of poly-crisis."

—Klaus Tilmes, *Former Director, Trade and Competitiveness Global Practice, World Bank*

Contents

About the Author

Dr. Nagy K. Hanna is global expert on digital economy, national innovation, smart cities, and public and business digital transformation strategies. He is advisor, educator, author, and thought leader on digital policies, institutions, and strategies. He has 5 decades of experience in advising policy makers in developing policies and institutions in support of digital economy. He worked with public, private, and civil society leaders to promote digitally-enabled innovation and transformation in various economic sectors and geographic regions. He was the World Bank's first senior advisor on digital economy.

While a senior staff of the World Bank, spanning 30 years, he appraised and managed many World Bank-funded digital innovation, technical education, and institutional development/capacity building programs. He was the lead corporate strategist of the World Bank. He pioneered the Bank's advisory services and lending for integrated digital transformation programs. He task managed World Bank assistance for India's first strategy for exporting software services. He founded and chaired a global forum on promoting digital innovation economies and building digital leadership institutions. He started his career with a focus on innovation and technology transfer, giving testimony to the United States House of Representatives on International Science and Technology Transfer Act.

He advises countries and aid agencies on developing institutions and leadership capabilities for integrating digital transformation programs into national development strategies. He was a visiting professor at Wits

University, South Africa, and a senior fellow and board member at the Center for Policy on Emerging Technologies. He co-founded People-Centered Internet, a global forum for inclusive Internet. He advised the US Government Office of Science and Technology on national competitiveness strategy, and on the editorial boards of several journals on science, technology, and innovation. He published extensively on digital economy policies and institutions, and the role of government and aid agencies in the digital age. He holds advanced executive development degree from Harvard and PhD degree from University of Pennsylvania.

CHAPTER 1

The Global, Technological, and Institutional Contexts

Abstract This chapter covers the broad global economic and technological contexts for development practice and the evolving role of aid agencies, particularly the World Bank. Countries and aid agencies have a chance to "do development right" and leapfrog old technologies and entrenched practices. Can digital solutions enable a cleaner and leaner lifestyle? Can smart cities and smart infrastructures lead to better capacity for adaptation and resilience, and at the same time, higher productivity?

Conceptions of economic development are changing due to the digital revolution. Traditional economic sectors are being transformed by digital technologies and the use of digital data. Changes in the global development environment call for a truly knowledge-based learning organization. This chapter defines digital transformation as an ecosystem and as a process. It also introduces the World Bank as it aims to be an evolving, learning, knowledge-based aid agency.

Keywords Global challenges · Digital technology · Digital transformation · Economic development · World Bank

N. K. Hanna, *Economic Development in the Digital Age*,
https://doi.org/10.1007/978-3-031-54569-6_1

Challenges Facing Humanity

Today the world is facing many challenges to promote inclusive and sustainable development and avert associated risks and unintended consequences. Developing countries must reinvent public policies and strategies for digital transformation to tackle interrelated grand development challenges: growing poverty and inequality, hunger and food insecurity, jobs and unemployment, health and pandemics, life-long learning, governance and corruption, conflicts and security, and water scarcity and climate change. ICT is a general-purpose technology that can be harnessed to provide innovative and smart solutions across all these challenges. Understanding these risks and opportunities is critical to harnessing the ongoing technology revolution for development.

Countries and aid agencies have a chance to "do development right" and leapfrog old technologies and entrenched practices. Can digital solutions enable a cleaner and leaner lifestyle?

The potential continues to expand. Smart cities and smart infrastructures would lead to better capacity for adaptation and resilience, and at the same time, higher productivity. Remote sensing, weather monitoring, and artificial intelligence would be leveraged to minimize waste and protect vulnerable populations and the environment. Development practitioners and environmentalists would join hands by harnessing the digital revolution to make economic development and environmental concerns complementary.

Climate change is an overarching global challenge calling for a whole-of-government, whole-of-society, and whole-of-the-world approaches. The growing array of digital technologies may hold answers to this looming crisis through both adaptation and mitigation. The biggest impact digital technologies can have on climate change is to enable all other economic sectors to reduce their greenhouse gas emission, by innovating new technologies that are more energy efficient. Digital technologies can also play a key role in strengthening the adaptive capacity of the country by supporting the processes of data gathering, decision-making, coordination, implementation, monitoring, and evaluation by all stakeholders and across the whole economy. They can make communities more resilient to climate change through better access to timely information and responsive service delivery.

Pandemics are on the rise with global consequences. COVID-19 has disrupted our ways of work and living, especially in the developing world.

Digital technologies have proven immensely useful in reducing the health, social, and economic costs of the crisis. At the same time, the pandemic has exposed significant gaps in digital access which prevent the uptake of online service delivery and remote work. These gaps are likely to cause more income inequality and skewed wealth concentration within and across countries. Public policies and investments should help to bridge the digital divide between urban and rural, and address gender, income, and regional gaps. Should digital technologies prioritize health and human development?

The rise of inequality and political polarization has been closely linked to the growth of digital platforms, social media-driven misinformation, and information monopolies. These trends feed on each other. The digital universe can be socially governed to promote equity, mutual understanding, and peaceful coexistence. How can societies not fall prey to total digital business- and state-surveillance? Development practitioners need to develop digital services that promote social and economic resilience, government transparency, and social empowerment. Governments can catalyze digital technologies to ensure equitable access to public services and protect societies from associated risks. Would governments, aid agencies, and business associations work with civil society organizations to strengthen governance, empower the marginalized, and make public services work for the poor?

The Ukraine crisis is diverting much attention and resources away from the global challenges facing humanity and is causing an arms race, threatening a new Cold War. The Israeli-Palestinian conflict continues to flare up, with no desirable end in sight. Digital technologies have enabled a new generation of weapons amplifying the powers of chaos and destruction. Can the global community find a way to end wars and insist on the use of digital technologies for peaceful, resilient, and inclusive development?

Continued inflation and stagnation, growing debt burdens, geopolitical polarization, healthcare costs and pandemics, climate change, and other global challenges require collective action. These multiple crises are reinforcing each other and leading to a crisis in development itself. We may be facing a long period of global stagflation and extreme inequality pulling us further away from achieving the Sustainable Development Goals. We need a sense of "collective urgency". How can the development community help countries "build back better", for resilience and sustainability? We must devise new approaches and practices for development institutions to harness the digital revolution for inclusive global development.

Are we moving in the right direction? The COVID-19 pandemic brought 800 million new users online in two years. There are growing pressures for reforming the international finance institutions. The IMF is expanding its mandate of financial stability to address the interconnected causes of global health, climate change, and food crisis. The Bank and other aid agencies are called upon to collaborate and reexamine their roles focusing on scaling financial assistance to the heavily-indebted developing countries and helping to build a more resilient world economy. While acknowledging the challenges, I remain hopeful that aid agencies and national governments can work together to harness the digital revolution, empower innovation, and contribute to a peaceful and resilient world.

Evolving Concepts of Economic Development

In the 1960s and 1970s, economic development was conceived in terms of GDP growth and sectoral shifts from agriculture to industrial development. Development policy was dominated by "big push" planning and investment in physical infrastructure and urbanization. From the 1980s onward, a convergence of views on policy reforms—the Washington Consensus—emerged: fiscal discipline, outward-orientation, market primacy, liberalization, privatization, and deregulation. Eventually, there came a growing recognition that market-driven policies would be inadequate for sustainable and inclusive growth without effective governance and institutional reforms. Development policy had to include more emphasis on human resources, the social sector, environmental sustainability, and anti-poverty programs, as well as changes in socio-economic structures of the country fueled by various forms of capital beyond natural and financial: human, institutional, organizational, and social. Increasingly, other core sources of growth and development are being recognized: research and innovation, knowledge creation, informational and learning capabilities, and open data, among other intangible assets.

Today, the process of economic development is transformed by digital technologies. Rather than following blueprints and standard strategies, development is conceived as an interactive, adaptive, and multi-stakeholder process, refined by monitoring, experimentation, and learning.

Traditional economic sectors are being transformed by digital technologies and the use of digital data. Cities, transport, logistics, utilities, and other infrastructures are all becoming "smart". The digital revolution also allows leapfrog development stages: from traditional agriculture to modern services, for example, skipping industrialization altogether. Public services can be delivered through public–private partnerships enabled by digital infrastructures. The digital revolution is giving rise to entirely new economies: the data economy, the frictionless economy, the sharing economy, the knowledge economy, the innovation economy, the co-creation economy, the collaboration economy, the green economy, and the smart economy (Hanna 2016a, 2016b, 2016c).

Economic policies and strategies, including those concerned with technology and innovation, are crucial to driving the forces of change. Development strategies and processes are shaped and implemented by using data, knowledge, communication, participation, empowerment, evaluation, and learning. Digital technology plays a key role in facilitating and accelerating all these processes. It is a powerful driver for accelerated development. Development theory and practice cannot afford to miss out on the most pervasive and transformative technology of our time.

Revolutionary changes in communication, knowledge management, and learning technologies shape client demand for development assistance and create new opportunities for learning at the individual, institutional, local, and global levels. Development agencies and practitioners must accelerate their learning accordingly.

A Changing Development Environment

What are the key structural changes in the global development environment? First is the decentralization and democratization of information, knowledge and learning are occurring at all levels—enabled by faster processing, powerful search tools, instant feedback, artificial intelligence, social media, and other digital platforms. These technological capabilities enable new modes of learning, research, and collaboration. They are transforming knowledge-based organizations and their service delivery. Information, big data, and processed knowledge have become critical assets that must be mobilized for staff usage, client service, and organizational effectiveness.

Second, developing countries have taken different paths to development, at different speeds, and with different outcomes. They vary by income and include those who have graduated from Bank lending to become aid donors, middle-income countries, low-income countries, and poor and fragile states. They demand diversified development assistance services and customized solutions to match their initial conditions, capabilities, and aspirations. Aid agencies are pressed to provide cross-country experience, evidence-based advice, more timely interaction, adaptive learning practices, and tailored implementation.

Third, new actors have emerged at the global level, beyond multilateral and bilateral development aid and financing agencies. They offer opportunities for collaboration, differentiation, knowledge sharing, and strategic partnerships. My own experience at the Bank and UN organizations suggests that learning to collaborate does not come naturally to large organizations. Large bureaucracies need to cultivate the incentives and culture for such cross-boundary multi-stakeholder and multi-organizational learning. Recent advances in digital technologies can facilitate information sharing and knowledge partnerships. But much more organizational learning and behavioral changes will be needed to realize this potential, particularly in relatively new areas like digital transformation.

Fourth, development partners have emerged within countries. Engaging them can help create demand for good government, mobilize local resources, facilitate social learning, and nurture home-grown solutions. It is a challenge for governments and aid agencies to play a critical role in empowering these local actors. There is a growing realization that broad local engagement is key to building local learning capacity and sustainable development. The cross-cutting nature of digital transformation makes such engagement an inevitable necessity.

Fifth, global challenges are rising and requiring collective learning and coordinated responses. Global, regional, and local issues are deeply intertwined. They are changing our understanding of the development process. Climate change, pandemics, and financial crises are clear examples. They are challenging business-as-usual paradigms and global governance. Digital transformation raises many transboundary regional and global issues, ranging from governance of an open Internet, to cybersecurity, and novel issues such as political polarization and "post-truth" information. Digital technologies offer opportunities to cope with global challenges ranging from monitoring pandemics and vaccines collaboration, to monitoring the environment and smart use of energy and natural resources. They facilitate the formation of communities of practice and global knowledge networks.

These changes in the global development environment call for a truly knowledge-based learning organization. The WBG attempt to become a "knowledge Bank" launched under Wolfensohn in 1997 was greeted with a mixture of high expectations and skepticism. It did create communities of practice and global knowledge networks. But it was technology-driven and did not address the many behavioral barriers to institutional learning. To be sustainable and operationally effective, learning and knowledge management needs to be actively sponsored by top management and firmly embedded in the organization's operational work and culture. Digital transformation is impossible without organizational and cultural transformation, as my colleagues and I learned when we attempted to mainstream this new practice.

Defining Digital Transformation

We can define digital transformation to mean using digital technologies to initiate and support deep and sustainable change in structures and processes, modes of production and consumption, value creation from available resources, and/or substantial increases in access to data. It is carried out at many levels, including organizations, economic sectors, government functions, cities, communities, and whole economies. Much of the use of digital technologies is done by individuals and for specific applications or services. Let us focus on the restructuring of whole economies. The country-wide economy was my unit of analysis and engagement. This was a privileged entry point for development assistance.

Progressively, I shifted my perspective from focusing on ICT components of development projects or silos of sectoral applications to economy-wide deployment of digital technologies and building the ecosystems of digital transformation for whole economies. The foundations part of the ecosystem included the digital policies, institutions, capabilities, culture, and data and communications infrastructure. These foundations were not only necessary to secure the expected payoffs from growing investments in digital technology applications. They were essential to enable diverse innovations at the grassroots and national levels, led by government, business, and civil society. They are still growing as part of the transformation ecosystem, and in response to new digital technology innovations and capabilities.

This shift was informed by the experience of pioneering nations like Singapore. But it was not an easy shift to treat digital development as a strategic and cross-cutting dimension of development since this shift would threaten the status quo of sector silos and aid bureaucracies, as demonstrated in the India and Sri Lanka cases in my twin book on *Case studies in digital transformation*.

Digital transformation is not just about user access to technology. It is a learning process by the whole society, especially if its full benefits were to be reaped and shared. That requires policy, institutional, and ultimately cultural changes. It calls for a holistic approach to development that would help integrate the new technologies into development thinking and practice. It opens up development possibilities and accelerates organizational change and policy learning. Despite potentially superior payoffs from such integration, the case studies I share later demonstrate how incentives within aid agencies tend to reinforce a divide between development and technology policy specialists, and delay response to the imperatives of the digital age.

The ongoing digital revolution may be conceptualized in terms of sets of interrelated technologies that have come in two waves so far. An early wave brought the spread of computers, telecommunications reforms and privatization, reengineering government and business processes, development of databases, and introducing e-government and e-business applications. This wave may be dated to the late 1980s and was reflected in the Bank's portfolio primarily in terms of computerization components of development projects. Much of the Bank's digital transformation assistance portfolio was driven by this wave.

The recent wave of digital technologies, starting around the beginning of the twenty-first century, generates and integrates data from all types of sources and uses artificial intelligence (AI) to detect patterns, generate content, and assist in decision-making. This wave is driven by instrumentation and data capturing (sensors, digital platforms, big data), ubiquitous connectivity (smart mobile, broadband), and intelligence (analytics, machine learning). It is also fueled by ubiquitous smart phones, converging data standards, social networks, crowdsourcing platforms, digital commerce, and cloud computing. The GPT of today goes beyond automation and substitution: it deals with intangibles—data, ideas, knowledge, communication, and learning. The AI revolution is the latest wave of the digital revolution and builds on the common foundations of an evolving digital ecosystem.

This pace of technological change is unprecedented in the global history of technology. Its impact, however, is uneven, mainly due to the gap between the rapidly evolving technologies, on the one hand, and the lagging political and administrative institutions, on the other hand. The pace of digital change is forcing countries to update their development strategies to leverage digital innovations and new technologies. Effective adoption of these technologies by institutions and societies requires significant investment in skills and changes in mind-set, roles, business processes, and working environments. It is important that all stakeholders have the incentives to make these investments.

Why Digital Transformation?

My research and work experience, and a fast-growing literature on innovation and economic transformation, convinced me that technological and institutional changes were fundamental to inclusive growth and poverty reduction. The rapid diffusion of digital technology and its impact on institutional change presented a unique opportunity for developing countries to accelerate economic transformation while promoting transparency, empowerment, and inclusion. I saw the Bank best positioned to leverage this general-purpose digital technology for shared prosperity at a global scale. Despite modest beginnings, I hoped to become a change agent to make it happen.

In my mind, I saw a parallel between the industrial revolution and the information technology revolution and the profound impact of this latest revolution we are currently living on economic transactions, industries, services, skills, markets, institutions, and societies. Much can be learned from examining these revolutionary consequences. The "invisible hand" of the market is being transformed or replaced by digital platforms. The ongoing technology revolution demands examining our basic assumptions about how the world works—economies, institutions, societies. It demands anticipating, experimenting, and learning about policies to influence this transforming global environment for the benefit of all.

To be effective, development practitioners need to be able to learn from the past, as well as to imagine the future. Yet many consider the past obsolete and irrelevant in addressing technological change. My story suggests otherwise. Economic historians like to theorize about major changes in techno-economic paradigms of the past driven by general-purpose technologies (GPTs) and the profound economic and institutional upheavals that they caused.[1] Information technology is the GPT or the most disruptive technology of our time. It challenges development practices. Learning from past GPT disruptions is critical to translating digital technologies into economic competitiveness and shared prosperity today.

I learned to appreciate the various roles that digital technologies have been playing in transforming economic sectors and institutions, and more recently in capturing, processing, and sharing data and embedding intelligence into all kinds of infrastructures and services. They are crucial for sustainable development, in all contexts and at all stages of the development process (World Bank 2016; Hanna 1993, 2009; Gurin 2013).

Digital transformation can provide an opportunity to get the country's elite to strike a "development bargain" (Dercon 2022). Political leaders would be open to policy and institutional reforms if these reforms would enable their countries to participate in the digital revolution and reap substantial digital dividends. I experienced this first-hand in my discussions with leaders in the public, private, and civil society sectors. The digital revolution raises new aspirations and possibilities to leapfrog, modernize, and accelerate the economic development process. It can help build an attractive vision of development for both the elites and society at large.

Artificial intelligence (AI) is rapidly emerging as a powerful new wave or set of tools for leveraging data and intelligence for development. AI has been driven by rapidly increasing amount of accessible digital data, advances in machine learning algorithms, and more powerful processing power, and the expansion of broadband networks and digital platforms. For some forecasters, AI, combined with other widely diffused digital transformation tools, is expected to become the most powerful engine for prosperity in history.

But the risks and challenges AI will pose are becoming clear too. Some of these risks are likely to be existential. Yet, so far development of AI remains heavily concentrated in a few advanced economies. AI is heavily dependent on the rest of digital transformation foundations, including enabling data sharing policies and the local data science and innovation

[1] General-purpose technologies (GPTs) are technologies that can affect an entire economy. GPTs have the potential to drastically alter societies through their impact on pre-existing economic and social structures. See, for example, Carlota Perez (2002).

system. The emerging AI divide can also exacerbate inequality within societies. AI will likely create upheaval in the workforce. AI will no longer be limited to big tech companies.

Predictive AI uses patterns from the past to predict the future. In medicine, for example, predictive AI is already spreading in advanced countries, used for patient-centered treatment, augmenting diagnosis, and tailoring treatment. On the other hand, generative AI generates advanced content in response to prompts from users. It presents novel challenges. Together with social media, generative AI will make it tougher to tell facts from fiction. It can become a threat to democracy and free markets. It can be used for state and business surveillance. These challenges will demand both local and global responses. Like any tool, both types of AI must be studied rigorously and deployed carefully. They must be added to the digital transformation ecosystem.

My advocacy for digital transformation should be put in perspective. Data, knowledge, and communication are present in one form or another in any development process. The digital revolution is impacting almost all forms of production, consumption, learning, and social life. Yet, digital transformation is not the sole solution for everything or can be treated as such in isolation. It is a profound, technologically driven force for change. It must be complemented by other socio-technical changes and adapted to local contexts to produce smart solutions to global and local challenges. It must be complemented by relevant policies, institutions, skills, and new ways of doing business to produce the desired outcomes.

Despite versatility and universality of digital technologies, country context matters. The payoffs are not automatic or deterministic. For the fragile and low-income countries, digital technologies hold much promise of substantial increases in productivity, resilience, public services, and technological leapfrogging. But they also bring to countries novel risks and vulnerabilities such as digital exclusion, surveillance, monopolies, misinformation, and costly unrealized benefits. The roles of ICT multinationals and aid agencies vary accordingly. For middle-income countries, the digital sector offers major opportunities for quality jobs, exports, and enhanced services and quality of life. Socio-economic context and country development priorities must shape and give directions to digital transformation.

Learning Journey at the Bank

When I joined the World Bank in 1975, it was a challenge to bridge the gap between mainstream development economists and technology policy specialists, and this gap remains to this day.[2] Through hands-on development assistance projects, I saw how information and communication systems can act as a powerful enabler and transformer for individuals, institutions, and economies. At the Indonesia Resident Mission, I observed the process of technical assistance and knowledge transfer, and the role of information in managing development projects and formulating evidence-based policies. I began to think of development as essentially a learning and empowerment process, enabled by information, communication, and knowledge—an idea that shaped my career choices at the Bank and beyond.

In 1987, I was appointed chief information policy officer and observed how information resources are shared and used to manage and exercise power across the Bank. The new technologies were changing the roles and capabilities of managers and staff, and the quality of interactions with country counterparts and other development partners. The Bank was being transformed slowly into a Knowledge Bank.

At the same time, I began to study where and how ICTs were part of Bank-funded development projects—with growing payoffs and risks. Institutions, industries, financial services, and whole economies were undergoing transformation with digital technologies. My advocacy of applying digital technologies in development crystalized when I formed a Bank-wide network that articulated the role of the Bank in the digital age. During 1990, I collaborated with 40 staff and first line mangers who volunteered their lunch time and helped me draft a "staff manifesto" for the Bank to proactively respond to the digital revolution.[3] Despite repeated presentations, senior management was not ready to respond.

[2] Depending on the context, the Bank refers to the World Bank's Board of Executive Directors, senior managers, front line managers, and/or the operational staff. For the purpose of this book, the Bank includes IBRD (International Bank for Reconstruction and Development, for middle-income countries) and IDA (the International Development Association for low income countries). The World Bank Group (WBG) refers to the two main organizations, the World Bank and the International Finance Corporation (IFC).

[3] Hanna, 1990, 1991.

Over time, I also began to realize that the digital revolution can have negative consequences unless strategically driven and harnessed for inclusive development. A neoliberal approach of market fundamentalism would only exacerbate the rising inequality within and across countries. Developing countries would also miss important opportunities to harness this general-purpose technology to advance health, education, and human development more broadly. They would miss out on advancing financial inclusion, connecting and empowering small enterprises, and serving isolated communities. I thought the Bank should also help countries minimize the growing risks of digital disruptions, structural unemployment, and climate change.

Progressively, I shifted my perspective from focusing on ICT components of development projects to economy-wide deployment of digital technologies and building the foundations of digital transformation for whole economies. These foundations were not only necessary to secure the expected payoffs from growing investments in digital technologies as components of development projects. They were essential to enable diverse innovations at the grassroots and national levels, led by government, business, and civil society. This shift was informed by the experience of pioneering nations like Singapore. But it was not an easy shift to treat digital development as a strategic and cross-cutting dimension of development since this shift would threaten the status quo of aid bureaucracies and sector silos, as demonstrated in later chapters on India and Sri Lanka.

Working with digital pioneers like Singapore and India during the 1990s, I observed the transformational power of digital technologies and felt very strongly that developing countries could not afford to miss out on harnessing these powerful technologies for sustainable development and poverty alleviation. Helping countries to leapfrog to the digital economy became the leitmotif of my work, sometimes exhilarating, at other times heartbreaking, but always worth the effort. Over the years, the intrinsic rewards of fulfilling my calling while working on innovative and learning-intensive tasks would usually outweigh the frustration of coping with a risk-averse bureaucracy.

Most recent in my journey, I could conceive of a major paradigm shift in development practice that would generate and use digital data to localize development and empower communities in pursuit of Sustainable Development Goals (SDGs). Prevailing information "poverty" in developing countries would be replaced by shareable data and information "rich" environment—enabled by digital technology. Digital technology applications in government, business, and civil society would augment policy learning and decision-making at all levels of institutions. Widening the scope of digitalization, combined with social media and open data policies would further broaden participation of society in their own local development. The binding constraints to realizing this vision will be the digital literacy and informational capabilities of society and its institutions.

An Evolving Learning Bank

In FY2022, Bank lending has reached US$115 billion.[4] These financial transfers to developing economies further leverage multiple orders from private investors and other aid agencies. The knowledge and technical assistance that are transferred as part of the development projects and investments are just as important. In the course of the last 50 years or so, the Bank has expanded its mandate beyond financing large complex infrastructure projects to diverse modes of assistance covering almost all economic sectors, policy reforms, and knowledge transfer. President McNamara was most influential in expanding assistance to the poor, the social sectors, and the poorest regions. The emphasis was on reaching ambitious lending targets. Over time, the Bank has expanded its coverage of assistance to almost all economic sectors of client countries.

As of 2022, these sectors were organized around the following global practices: agriculture; education; energy; environment; finance, competitiveness and innovation; governance; health, nutrition and population; human development; jobs; macroeconomics, trade and investment; poverty; social protection; inclusion; urban, disaster and resilience; transport; digital development; and water. Some of these are sectors, others cut across several sectors, and others yet are important themes like poverty and the environment. Collaboration across these global practices proved difficult and recent attempts have been made to reorganize and consolidate them into fewer practices.

The Bank's internal organization has evolved from centralized projects departments and country programs to a complex matrix organization with global practices (each composed of several economic sectors), on the one hand, and regions (composed of country management units),

[4] World Bank Group commitments (including short-term finance, mobilization and Recipient-Executed Trust Funds) rose to $115 billion in fiscal year 2022 (July 2021–June 2022), or $5.3 billion higher than FY21.

on the other hand. Staffing also shifted from primarily mid-career and seasoned technical specialists and managers to macroeconomists, generalists, researchers, and short-term consultants. The management and administrative budget, together with much of headquarters staff, have been also decentralized to field offices in client countries. Decentralization was made possible with the major advances in telecommunication technologies. Still much of the decision-making authority remained at headquarters, since the broad directions and major commitments are determined and approved by the Board of Directors of the Bank, representing the ministries of finance of member countries. IFC, the private arm of the WBG, has undergone similar decentralization reforms.

The shifts in the Bank's roles and processes were in part driven by the rapid changes in digital technologies from mainframe and stand-alone computers to networked computers and commercial Internet, to mobile communications and smart phones, to digital platforms, big data and artificial intelligence, to smart cities and intelligent infrastructures, and so on. Organizational shifts were slow and partial, as they were constrained by WBG governance, the politics of major shareholders, the perceived need for confidentiality, and the need for consensus among large number of shareholder countries.

A major change occurred in the Bank's products and services portfolio, venturing beyond project lending to policy lending and diverse analytical and advisory services. This shift was driven by the changing conceptions of economic development and frequent debt crises. Structural adjustment lending (SAL) and subsequently development policy finance (DPF) instruments were developed to provide fast disbursements that contribute to a nation's budget in support of government's policies and institutional reforms. Progressively, DPF operations were programmed over time to secure sustained ownership by government to address difficulties in implementing policy reforms during debt crises.

I define digital transformation here to be about using digital technologies to initiate and support deep and sustainable change in structures and processes, modes of production and consumption, value creation from available resources, and/or substantial increases in access to data. It is carried out at many levels, including organizations, economic sectors, government functions, cities, communities, and whole economies.

The country was my unit of analysis and engagement and my privileged entry point for development assistance. Much of the use of digital technologies is done by individuals and for specific applications or services.

However, I focus here on the restructuring of whole economies. I believe economy-wide perspective would best capture the policy and institutional foundations of digital transformations and their productivity impact.

Digital transformation is not just about user access to technology. It is a learning process by the whole society, especially if its full benefits were to be reaped and shared. That requires policy, institutional, and ultimately cultural changes. It calls for a holistic approach to development that would help integrate the new technologies into development thinking and practice. It opens up development possibilities and accelerates organizational change and policy learning. Despite potentially superior payoffs from such integration, the case studies I share later demonstrate how incentives within aid agencies tend to reinforce a divide between development and technology policy specialists, and delay response to the imperatives of the digital age.

While the Bank has not been as effective and innovative as it would like to proclaim, it has stood the test of time, adapting and swaying with the wind of changing fashions of development thinking. At different times, it emphasized poverty alleviation, rural and urban development, structural adjustment, Washington consensus, good governance, Sustainable Development Goals (SDGs), climate change, and global public goods. It also had to respond to many shareholders and stakeholders, with conflicting agendas. My hope is that it would continue to reform and learn, in response to the multiple crises at hand and the opportunities opened up by the digital revolution.

Today, the Bank and other aid agencies need to address multiple, overlapping global crises, ranging from global pandemics to refugees, from failed states to climate change. Its clients are also dealing with growing debt, inequalities, and hunger. These challenges now require more than investments at scale. They demand new mind-sets, knowledge, learning, and innovation capabilities to harness the ongoing technological revolution and leapfrog toward smart, inclusive, and sustainable global development. The digital revolution offers new and powerful tools to respond to these multiple crises—not a substitute for traditional sectors and short-term financial infusions, but to rebuild back smarter, longer-term solutions.

My work on strategic planning further deepened my appreciation for the limitations of strategic management at global development institutions. Management of strategic issues at such institutions is fraught with difficulties: transparency, accountability, powerful egos and turfs, and difficult-to-reach consensus among competing shareholders. I learned to appreciate how difficult it is to harness the enormous capacities of large multi-stakeholder institutions to serve the needs of diverse client countries. I learned to apply planning tools to manage strategic issues at the Bank and country digital transformation strategies. At times, "strategic ambiguity" was the most attractive course of action for the Bank's top management and governing Board.[5] But such ambiguity often led to "strategic" inaction, or it was used to avoid making strategic choices.

Throughout my Bank career, I faced institutional hurdles that penalized staff for pursuing transformational projects, in general, and for working on mainstreaming digital transformation, in particular. I was not always alone in such battles, but I lost many like-minded colleagues along the way when they gave up and left the Bank's service. I had to switch roles and assignments but remained employed at the Bank—moving from country assistance management, to public sector management, to private sector development, to corporate strategy, to development assistance evaluation, and to technology transfer and digital transformation. I had to reinvent myself and accept risks to my career that come with pioneering or innovating new fields or modalities of development assistance. I learned to live with uncertainty.

Large aid agencies face many learning obstacles. These learning disabilities often led to significant delays in the Bank responding to opportunities and threats, innovating solutions and entering new fields of assistance. Often, the Bank chose to ignore the most difficult needs of client countries so as to minimize reputational risks. Aversion to acknowledging and addressing the growing risks of the digital revolution may have delayed the Bank's response to surveillance and cybersecurity, for example. In the Bank hierarchy, new areas of assistance or innovation could only be sustained when safely introduced by top management. Unfortunately, this top-down strategy meant a delayed response, and such delayed response to the digital revolution is unlikely to be a viable or acceptable strategy to minimize risk and maintain development effectiveness.

Accelerated organizational learning at aid agencies will be necessary to meet the challenges of inclusive growth and poverty elimination, and the challenges of climate change and global public goods. This active learning

[5] The WBG is governed by a board that represents 190 countries. The more innovative the strategies being proposed, the more difficult the Bank's consensus and decision-making.

will demand broadening the mission of aid agencies and international finance institutions. It will require both continuing evolution and strategic reform. The digital revolution offers new tools and opportunities to meet these challenges as it provides smart solutions that optimize the use of energy, infrastructure, water, and financial and natural resources. It offers dramatic improvements in productivity, resilience, governance, and public and private services. It presents novel risks to individuals, communities, countries, and humankind.

Ignoring the digital revolution is not an option for the developing world. In following chapters and case studies, I trace the Bank's early responses of denying the relevance and priority of responding to the digital revolution. Influential economists have argued that governments have no role to play, suggesting that the Bank has no role or comparative advantage, and/or highlighting the reputational risks of entering a new field of development assistance. While acknowledging the unintended or inevitable risks, I argued that the biggest and most likely risk for late adopters would be inertia and vested interests against change. The Bank cannot be just reactive or the "last resort" for financing development.

There is a lot at stake here when we think about the future of global development. We have the opportunity to develop nations by giving them innovative technologies from which to build. Could the World Bank and other aid agencies rise to the challenge? To do this, they need to work hard to fit the digital age. Without working to fit in this system, they run the risk of losing power and becoming irrelevant. There is hope that they can partner with global and local stakeholders and harness the power of the ongoing digital revolution.

CHAPTER 2

Motivations

Abstract This chapter outlines the author's motivations to write a book on digital transformation informed by practice. The author reflects upon his motivations to write this book in light of the many challenges facing humanity today. It covers his early encounters with poverty in Egypt, Sudan, India, Sri Lanka, Palestine, and elsewhere.

Keywords Poverty · Egypt · Motivations · Memoir · World Bank

Motivations

In my research and experience, I adopted a participant-observer methodology. I draw on my experience as active participant in development assistance, and on observing other participants and partners in the development assistance and digital transformation practice. The aim is to offer both past and emerging lessons learnt from pioneering and practicing digital transformation by policy makers and development partners.

The current and looming crises of climate change, growing inequality, dehumanizing poverty, unsustainable debts, and threats to democracy and governing must be matched by humankind capacity for adaptation, innovation, and learning. Much has been written, by others, and my own (Hanna 1993, 2009, 2010, 2011, 2016; World Bank 2016)

N. K. Hanna, *Economic Development in the Digital Age*,
https://doi.org/10.1007/978-3-031-54569-6_2

on specific applications and innovations in digital technologies that can support adaption and learning to eliminate global poverty and sustain a healthy planet. Fortunately, the revolutionary advances in digital technologies can help optimize the development and use natural and human resources to create smart cities, smart energy, smart infrastructure, smart finance, smart public services, and smart education and health, among others. This book focuses instead on how to make this desirable future happen through policy and cultural changes in the Bank, aid agencies, and developing countries. It aims at addressing the enabling policy and cultural environment necessary to invent both country-focused and global solutions for smart development.

My research into digital transformation aims to go beyond the walls of academia. It aims to inform decision-making in countries and in international finance institutions. It aims at empowering development practitioners and reformers to improve digital development practice. Country experiences and those of development partners are examined to further develop the frameworks, tools, and processes that would advance both digital development theories and practices.

This book is an outcome of "implementation research". It goes beyond the rhetoric and self-reporting of aid agencies, governments, and technology companies. There is a huge gap between these polished reports and their promises, on the one hand, and actual implementation and transformational results on the ground. The book focuses on the *processes* of digital diagnosis, strategy formulation, and strategy implementation, adaptation, evaluation, and learning. It shows how to gain value from these processes. Outcomes are shaped by the design of these processes. The book tries to understand the interactions between aid agencies and governments, between government and business, and between external advisors and local doers. It examines how diagnostic tools are applied and reshaped by the context and the user. The outcomes of these tools and models should go beyond measurements and data. They should help secure inclusive participation, build local ownership, and form coalitions for sustainable reform.

This book is part autobiographical and part polemical about harnessing the digital revolution by countries, aid agencies, and development practitioners. I share my long struggles for reforming and innovating development practice—primarily concerning the challenges and opportunities arising from the recent digital revolution—in the pursuit of the mission of eliminating global poverty and securing inclusive and sustainable prosperity. I draw on real-world examples of barriers to change that I and other practitioners encountered, and on ways of making progress in spite of them. I share how my ideas and conceptional frameworks of development have evolved through implementation research and co-learning with client countries.

While writing this book I was conflicted between recalling my professional journey into economic development and my personal journey through life and its diverse and unplanned experiences. In the end, I limited sharing my personal life only to those critical events that motivated me to write and practice development assistance and digital transformation. I did not do justice to capturing the autobiographical parts, as I aimed for wide sharing of lessons I learned about development. Missing in this, my family life and all the art and artifacts of the world, all the people I came across who had no direct links with my profession, and all the miracles of life that enriched me and gave me deeper meaning and appreciation for life lived fully. Documenting my professional journey was enough of a challenge that it demanded another companion book.

My view of development has been shaped by my early personal experience decades ago, emphasizing a holistic approach, sustainability, and inclusiveness. My early experiences also influenced my approach to development assistance practice—promoting client-centric ownership, empowerment, leadership, innovation, and learning. This book is my personal take on the evolution of the digital development practice at the World Bank up to, and including 2022. My experience has been shaped by the institutional conditions within which I operated, mainly of the Bank and its interactions with client countries. The book deals with digital development strategies and practices at the Bank's corporate, country, and project levels. It focuses on the key events of my learning journey and the lessons I took away that may be helpful to advancing a new development practice at the World Bank Group (WBG), other aid agencies, and client countries.

There is a great need to leverage the ongoing technological revolution for economic development. The Bank and other aid agencies took a very long time to recognize the importance of the digital revolution and to respond in a timely and effective manner to the challenges and opportunities presented by this new techno-economic paradigm.

As I worked across many economic sectors and different departments within the Bank, I tried to build bridges between two separate camps:

digital technology specialists and mainstream development practitioners. The new language of ICT specialists was often incomprehensible to mainstream development practitioners. Digital technology specialists were early believers in the power of their new digital tools. Mainstream economists, on the other hand, were skeptical. They viewed technology as a black box. They often held the stereotype that ICT specialists are narrowly focused on technology as an end in itself. My experience working with the technology specialists, who were dedicated to digital technology for development, had a much broader and contextual view of technology adoption. They often held advanced degrees in social or physical sciences, beyond engineering. And even though it was clear that this technological revolution was too important to be left for the technologists alone to deploy, hybrid staff who could bridge the two camps faced many barriers to pursuing cross-disciplinary careers in the traditional sectoral siloes of the Bank and other aid agencies.

My experience emphasizes the importance of integrating country development strategies (demand side) with ICT strategies and applications (supply side). It suggests ways to bring the two sides together into a dynamic ecosystem. Country cases demonstrate that there are many lessons to be learned from the rich experiences of pioneering countries. No one-size fits all. This is a new field of development assistance with much to explore across countries at different levels of technology adoption and economic performance.

I also hope to help accelerate the learning curve of countries and aid agencies in leveraging digital transformation for development. Developing countries and aid agencies stand at an inflection point: disruptive technologies, primarily digital and data-driven, are creating new opportunities for growth, productivity, and inclusion. Given the pace of technological change, national governments, aid agencies, and new actors in development must accelerate their learning and develop effective collaboration strategies.

My journey was driven, above all, by my passion for addressing development challenges through powerful new tools offered by revolutionary advances in digital technologies. This has been a quest to understand and transform development through the use of digital technologies. Often, I had to play two roles: broad development strategist (formal role) and digital policy specialist and advocate (informal role). The second role was not adequately budgeted or sanctioned by senior management.

Without passion for innovating development solutions, I would not have endured the resistance and setbacks I faced working in a large, risk-averse bureaucracy. The educational conversation with client countries was more than adequate reward to sustain my journey. I chose digital transformation as a field of development practice not because it is easy and familiar, but because it is hard and less traveled. It is a new terrain open for learning, discovery, and innovation. I believed it would test the Bank's capabilities for strategic adaptation and sustained learning. And, I believed, it was consequential for all other fields of development.

The lessons I learnt in the course of my career inform the suggestions I propose in this book. How can aid agencies better prepare for the digital age? I focus on the World Bank not just because this is where I spent years learning about development, both at the corporate strategy level and at the frontline in the field, but also because the Bank is the largest aid agency, with resources, talent, and capacity to mobilize capital markets and donor trust funds to serve developing countries. The Bank has demonstrated its effectiveness in delivering technical and financial assistance in traditional lending areas, such as physical infrastructure and policy reform, but it has yet to master digital development to help governments compete in the digital age. And it is facing serious learning challenges in mastering this paradigm shift.

But my most powerful motivation to write this book is my deep passion to help alleviate extreme poverty and suffering—a passion shaped by the personal experiences of my childhood and youth. To me, writing this personal journey is an act of love: love for the impoverished and disempowered, for my fellow travelers who challenge aid agencies to fulfill their promise, and for country policy makers and reformers who meet development transformation challenges on the ground. It is also an act of hope that my experience will be of value to the younger generation of development practitioners.

Early Encounters with Poverty

My first encounter with poverty was back in my childhood in Egypt. When my father died of a heart attack at the age of 40, our life became much harder. My mother had to navigate and bribe Egyptian bureaucracy to receive pension support to raise her four children. The frequent food shortages in 1960s Egypt made life even more difficult. With no connections with the right people, we waited in long lines for the most basic goods. Later on, as a Sunday school teacher in my teens, I would often visit my students, many living in poor communities and slums, some working as child laborers. I witnessed child abuse and violence against women, especially in low-income communities. The suffering and hunger of those children stayed with me for life. To me those were real people suffering, not just government statistics. That was when I first felt it was my life's mission to get involved in poverty alleviation and development.

Growing up in Egypt, I first saw poverty's ugly face in the poor neighborhoods of Cairo, and later, when working in the Sudan. My heart was with the dispossessed. My siblings used to taunt me for fighting for the underdog, even when the prospects of winning were slim. Ever since, I felt a strong urge to dedicate myself to poverty alleviation.

My world view was shaped by Egypt's experience under President Nasser: the revolution against imperialism and the emergence of a socialist state. The ills of Western imperialism were repeatedly articulated at school. I learned how debt was an instrument of the 1882 British colonial conquest of Egypt. In my high school history class, I read about revolutions in the US, France, and the rest of Europe, the scientific revolution, and the struggle to establish secular governments.

I vividly recall how vulnerable I felt as a child when British, French, and Israeli military jets roared over me in 1956—as the allies invaded Egypt after the nationalization of the Suez Canal. For many Egyptians, Israel was an agent of Western imperialism. At the time, Egypt was a leader in the global non-aligned movement. It saw the World Bank as a tool of US imperialist ideology, especially after the Bank refused to finance the high dam (due to US government objection). Later I also read about the "white man's burden" and the "civilizing mission" of Western imperial dominance that may have shaped the tools and modalities of development assistance.

I was so affected by the suffering and pain of these communities that even my faith in God faltered. How could a loving God permit or cause such suffering? Formal religious institutions were unable to provide adequate answers. I wrote to God, spent time in a monastery, talked with mystics and the Pope of Alexandria, and read both religious and secular existential philosophy, searching for answers. Perhaps my religious zeal fueled my passion to help reduce poverty and promote social and economic justice.

And the more I traveled in poor and underdeveloped areas around the world working on projects like slum upgrading in Indonesia and rural development in India, the more motivated I felt to devote myself to this field.

While at Cairo university, I was attracted to socialism, with its emphasis on economic justice and equitable access to free education and health services. It fit my yearning for equality, human dignity, and addressing basic human needs. I considered democracy to be a luxury when a significant part of the population went hungry. I despised the class structure as much as authoritarianism.

Later, I saw the excesses and corruption of Egypt's bloated public sector, the failures of army-led industrialization and the debacle of crony capitalism. My studies in industrial organization and engineering convinced me that Egypt was on the wrong track. I saw idle assets and mismanaged factories in army-led public enterprises. On a student exchange program in Germany, I understood the importance of technology and management for learning to compete. It took cumulative technological and managerial learning to industrialize.

I was most attracted to social sciences and humanities even while studying the dry subjects of engineering and mathematics. At that time, engineering was celebrated in Egypt as the top profession of choice in support of Egypt's independence and Nasser's ambitious plans for industrialization. But, at the same time, I was hungry for knowledge to answer existential questions concerning the meaning of life and the human condition. I read in search of the unity of knowledge across all disciplines. I found my moments of happiness and peak experience through reading. I used my meager allowance to buy and devour used books in all subjects. Then, there were no public libraries or Internet to access.

I was fortunate to attend a government-funded boarding school for the most talented students in the country. This helped me avoid both the deterioration of Egyptian public schools as well as the elitism of its private schools. It also saved me from the prevailing emphasis on rote learning in these schools that took all the fun and joy out of learning. I dreamt of becoming the Minister of Education so I could reform the education system. But I felt I owed my excellent education to the poor workers of Egypt. Being unable to repay them by reforming the Egyptian education system, I turned my attention to practicing inclusive development through the World Bank.

My decision to immigrate to the US was not a simple one as I deeply valued my cultural heritage and personal connections in Egypt. In my first job after graduating, I tried to investigate corruption in the public sector and was rewarded by death threats. It quickly became clear that as a member of the minority Egyptian Christian community, I would be more vulnerable than most if I were to continue to advocate for reform and transparency. Also, the war with Yemen in 1964 and with Israel in 1967 had drained the Egyptian economy and dimmed the prospects for recent engineering graduates. And as a student of economics and engineering, I felt that Egypt's industrialization strategy was bound to fail: the government ignored the role of the market and the country's comparative advantages. In joining the Bank, I was full of hope and ambition that I could be in a position to help developing countries around the world to address development challenges similar to those Egypt was struggling with.

My trip to West Germany through a student exchange program was one more experience that inspired me to emigrate after my graduation. As a student, I was already aware of the technological advances of the West. I took advantage of this student exchange program to get an invitation to work with a large wood-processing corporation in Rosenheim, Bavaria. As I started to work, I realized the job was not what has been stated in my contract. The actual work was manual and involved handling heavy machinery and inhaling wood dust, with few health safeguards. Two weeks later I was fired. I felt relieved. I also realized that the industrial might of 1965 Germany was largely driven by the low-cost guest workers from Turkey and Italy. These workers spent evenings at the local bars, drowning their sorrows in German beer. I understood then what Marx meant by worker alienation and the fate of the proletariat.

Soon after, I was lucky to find a job with AEG Telefunken's design office that better fit my engineering background. This time I not only enjoyed my work but explored art museums, traveled through West and East Germany, and wandered in the famous German forests. This was the first time in my life that I saw so many trees. I was smitten. I started to draw trees with an ink pen on random scraps of paper, trying to capture their unique beauty. I celebrated the dance of the trees, their fall and spring colors, the captivating mystery of forests—the Creator's living architecture. Nature's endless imagination is an inspiration and a challenge! **See drawings!**

Searching for the sky © Nagy Hanna

Dancing alone © Nagy Hanna

Dancing together © Nagy Hanna

Embrace © Nagy Hanna

I returned to Egypt, completed my studies, and applied for immigration to the US. The US government had revised its immigration policies to accept immigrant engineers and doctors from Egypt and other non-Western countries. It took me two years to prepare. I immersed myself into economics, philosophy, sociology, psychology, and the sciences. I took courses at the American University of Cairo in arts and languages. I was eager to embrace Western culture and delved into it with great enthusiasm.

At times of economic, political, and intellectual oppression, I always yearned for freedom. As part of the Coptic minority in Egypt, I felt disempowered and compelled to excel in education and later, to immigrate. I dreamt of a renaissance for Egypt and the Middle East.

I bid a tearful farewell to my family in March 1969, with a one-way ticket to the US in hand, leaving my siblings and mother with the hope of joining me one day, once I establish myself in the land of opportunity. Several friends from Cairo University were already there, struggling to establish themselves in different states around the country. I was the first in my extended family to emigrate, leaving for an uncertain future with only USD 100 in hand. But I knew that my family has pinned all their hopes on me, leaving me no choice but to succeed. Despite some trepidation, I was hopeful and full of ambition.

My first three years in Philadelphia were very demanding, as I worked as an industrial engineer during the day and studied for my masters during evenings and weekends. Working in the headquarters of a big US corporation, I felt pressured to deal with labor as a dispensable resource. I hated to be in this position, siding with management over labor. In the meantime, I understood how an information-rich environment can substantially enhance the productivity of a young engineer. It gave me a deeper appreciation of corporate governance, technology transfer, and cumulative technological learning within large corporations.

I planned to shift from engineering to medicine or social and economic studies. I completed pre-med studies and did research on the artificial heart for a Master's thesis. But I discovered I could not complete my studies for a medical degree without having to re-do all the university courses I had already taken in Egypt. However, I gained a new perspective from biological systems. The exposure to biomedical sciences and bio-engineering gave me valuable insights into new multidisciplinary fields. I began to see the complexity of the heart, the circulation system, the multiple feedback loops, and the biological processes as information processes that govern our bodies and environment.

Campus life at the University of Pennsylvania and the International House of Philadelphia was a great way to adapt to my new environment. Residents at the House were graduate students and researchers from all over the world. It was there that I met my future wife, Linda, who was completing her doctorate in Spanish literature and medieval art history. I thought her study of the past balanced out my focus on the future and such issues as the "Limits to Growth" and planning for the year 2000! At the International House and the University, we had a very rich social and intellectual life. Multicultural and multidisciplinary debates were complemented by weekend dancing.

Why the World Bank?

At the Wharton Business School at the University of Pennsylvania, I focused on decision sciences, institutional economics, economic modeling, systems theory, and socio-technical systems. I was lucky to contribute to a major economic planning study for the Sudan. It was technical assistance in action, where I was both participant and observer. I had the opportunity to make a presentation of this work on behalf of this poor country to the "rich and famous" World Bank—it was my first encounter with my future life-long employer. This study contributed to my PhD dissertation about the potential and limitations of quantitative decision-making and planning models and modalities of foreign technical assistance.

Later on, I was really moved by Robert McNamara, then Bank President, as I read speeches about dedicating the Bank to fighting urban and rural poverty.[1] His messages clicked with me. It was then that I realized that my dream of poverty alleviation could be fulfilled through a "reformed" Bank. This was the mission I was seeking. It gave meaning to my life.

Thus began my personal journey through a large elitist development bureaucracy. I believed in the Bank's mission, and I felt it had much of the resources and scale needed to address the challenges of global poverty. At

[1] Other leaders of the Bank also followed suit: Kim Jaycox on urban poverty, Monty Yudelman on rural poverty, Hollis Chenery on redistribution with growth, and Mahbub Ul Haq on basic needs, among others.

times, I clashed with the Bank's neoliberal—even neo-colonial—ideology. I criticized its structural adjustment binge that ignored human costs and sowed inequality. I felt sick to my stomach when some Bank colleagues acted as task masters in their "dialog" with the most vulnerable countries. The Bank remains the oldest and biggest development financier, but runs the risks of complacency, inertia, rigidity, and arrogance. The Bank was never a perfect development vehicle, and it failed more often than it cared to admit, yet it has the mandate, and at critical times demonstrated that it could learn and meet new challenges.

While at the Bank, I met colleagues with diverse values. Even though the dominant culture—relative to mine—was elitist, conservative, and risk averse, I met some innovative, dedicated, and caring individuals I loved working with. The Bank had many subcultures: from academic, financial, and bureaucratic to operational and even entrepreneurial. There were also various informal organizations and opportunities for thought leadership. I joined a unique network called the Friday Group, or Values in Development, where concerns about environment, social development, religious values, economic justice, corporate culture, corruption, and governance were freely discussed with eminent speakers, including the Bank President, social workers, and even nuns.[2] These people and groups helped me live with the conflict between my own values and the Bank's neoliberal policy agenda, competitive culture, and posh lifestyles.

Managerial Culture at World Bank

When I joined the Bank, McNamara was President. He was reshaping the Bank through changes in organizational structure, incentives, and a globally competitive Young Professionals program (YPs). I was not a perfect fit for the Bank. Yes, I joined others who came from similar elite US and UK educational institutions. I had graduated from the Wharton school, University of Pennsylvania, with a PhD in a multidisciplinary program covering strategy, operations research and systems science. I found the

[2] A founding member of the group was David Beckman, who later became the President of the *Bread for the World* NGO.

YP culture to be too careerist and elitist[3] as it prized academic credentials over commitment, experience, and empathy.

The YP program embodied McNamara's managerial style of selecting "the best and the brightest". There was the expectation, largely fulfilled, that YPs would fit into this management culture, and would quickly become senior managers at the Bank. McNamara served as President of the Bank from 1968 to 1981, long enough to leave a major imprint on the managerial culture of the Bank. This managerial culture put emphasis on analysis, numbers, rationality, certainty, efficiency (measured by standard lending coefficients), and having ready and clear answers to complex development problems. It was unforgiving of risk taking. Fear of failure was palpable. Information was hoarded. Information moved in silos upward for centralized decision-making. Decisions, initiatives, and innovations came from the top down. Procedures and documents were standardized and sanitized to create a certain internal reality that diverted from the external and uncertain reality of diverse client economies, institutions, and cultures.

The managerial culture of McNamara and the YP program had significant impact on Bank borrowers. Conforming to current fads and ideologies of development was more important for staff careers than responding to country specificity and experimenting and learning with the client. Staff had to manage the two realities, one for the field and the other for the Bank's Board—often giving priority to the sanitized and internally constructed reality. Writing reports for each other and providing elegant presentations were given a premium over practical advice and timely solutions that empower clients.

There were exceptions and challenges to this culture. I observed first-hand some client-centered team leaders (TTLs) who clearly engaged in a learning journey with their clients and at times had to challenge Bank orthodoxy. They were at their best when they were in the field. They often entered the Bank mid-career, after substantial field experience. They were seldom mobilized to mentor the YPs.

The YP administrator wrote in my closed performance evaluation file that I would not stay with the Bank for long, as I was inclined to challenge the bureaucracy and not live within its boundaries and constraints.

[3] The YP program was modeled at least implicitly after the elite civil services of some European countries. There was the expectation, largely fulfilled, that YPs would become the senior managers of the Bank.

Defying his prediction, I had to reinvent myself many times over to pursue creative roles while testing the boundaries set by the Bank's bureaucracy. Taking the Myers-Briggs personality test, I was typed as a highly intuitive and perceptive personality—an outlier for the Bank's conservative managerial culture that prized the analytical and judging types.

I believed that the key to professional effectiveness was to be client-centered—defining the problem and seeking the solution jointly with the client (Argyris and Schon 1974). At times, this meant putting the interests of the client above the need to maintain team harmony and abide to the bureaucratic status quo. It also often meant focusing on innovative tasks that could open up new possibilities for my development practice, even if it challenged the dominant way of doing business and risked my career. By doing so, I may have underestimated the strength of bureaucratic inertia and resistance to change and not given sufficient attention to understanding the caution and fears of my peers and managers, and the need to patiently invest in building coalitions for innovation and reform. Winning support for innovation in a hierarchical and risk-averse organization requires significant personal and team investment.

I joined the Bank at a time when McNamara was steering a fast-growing organization toward the mission of poverty alleviation and meeting basic needs, and expanding lending to social sectors, including education, health, population, and nutrition. I recall Bank staff presenting the first nutrition project in Indonesia to the Executive Directors with the expectation that it would boost labor productivity. It was necessary to justify these kind of social development projects first and foremost on economic grounds. The Bank was primarily a project financing organization. Rate of return was a key justification to investment lending. Project management skills were highly valued. The organizational structure was highly centralized. Bank processes were tailored in line with the blueprint design of engineering projects. Bank-funded projects were considered the "privileged particles of development"—with project implementation units that followed Bank procedures and safeguards. The very conception of development and consequently development assistance was being transformed, albeit slowly.

Learning is relational and contextual. I learned the most about development when I was on field missions, in close interaction with Bank teams and country clients. Field missions offered a close look at real development challenges and presented a learning environment free from the constraints of a centralized bureaucracy. Reduced hierarchy among mission team members, however temporary, as well as the intense interaction with country stakeholders in the local context were key to agile learning.

My convictions, sense of urgency, and empathy for those I encountered during country engagements often led me to challenge the "status quo" and the Bank's institutional rigidities. Some colleagues saw me as idealistic or perhaps not willing to compromise in order to stay in line with Bank norms and imperatives. I tried my best to be a change agent, a loyal critic. Concerns about country ownership and stakeholder empowerment (acting as a hand-holder) often conflicted with Bank leverage and donor conditionalities (task master). Some influential Bank economists felt obliged to compete with IMF staff where conditionality was in vogue. They were rewarded for highly critical policy reviews of their country counterparts. These reviews were influenced by internal peer-review standards and often distorted conceptions of professional excellence and effectiveness, where the Bank is the sole definer of the problem and solution (Argyris and Schon 1974).

The understanding of client country conditions (as internally constructed and shared within the Bank's headquarters) was often considered more important than the country field reality.[4] Field-oriented staff who excelled in serving their clients were suspected of "going native" and the results they delivered were often ignored by Bank management. Maybe this disconnect was caused by the domination of large Western shareholders, as well as the gap between Bank staff, mainly recruited from elite US and UK universities, and the poor they were expected to serve. I wondered. My empathy with the client drove me to learn more about country conditions and to view the country as a whole. I hoped a more accurate understanding of reality would emerge when profiles were co-created with in-country counterparts.

My convictions informed my sense of purpose, strengthened my commitment and resilience, and helped me overcome many institutional hurdles. What can be more important than eradicating extreme poverty and building a better future for mankind, I thought! It was a privilege to serve from a relatively comfortable and secure position, so why not take some career risks!

[4] Bank staff have to manage two realities, one when they are on mission interacting with clients in the field, while the other is a socially-constructed reality (sanitized reports) for senior management and the Board.

It was in 2004 that Jim Wolfensohn, World Bank President, a demanding development practitioner and banker, while chairing a Board meeting on the e-Lanka project that I presented, complimented us by saying: "I have waited 10 long years to see such a ground- breaking digital transformation project"; and added "I hope to see much more of such thought leadership". It was clear that when empowered, given adequate autonomy and allowed to co-create with clients, we were able to break through the bureaucracy, reconcile the recurring tensions between serving the Bank and the client country, and deliver exceptional results. Yet the personal costs incurred by the pioneers were high. The mainstreaming of the e-Sri Lanka innovations within the Bank was slow mainly due to turf conflicts, staff changes, misalignment across several managerial layers, and other institutional learning constraints. While such constraints are common across sectors and aid agencies, they tend to slow the pace of developmental learning and innovation at a time when the digital revolution and global development challenges are most pressing.

I often wondered if I was simply ahead of my time in pioneering digital transformation assistance at the Bank. Did I underestimate the personal risks and institutional constraints involved? Perhaps my zeal came across as too critical of the status quo. Perhaps I was a meddlesome intellectual gadfly in the eyes of more conservative managers. Maybe I was too impatient with the slow response of a large development bureaucracy. I tried to be a change agent and loyal critic.[5] After all, the Bank had substantial resources and talent, and often reacted to external criticism, albeit with some delay, as with adjustment lending and the impact of Bank-funded projects on the environment.

Are these words of despair? By no means! I loved the mission of development. I was fortunate to work for an influential organization with a mandate to fight global poverty. So far, the Bank proved indispensable during global financial crises, entered new fields of assistance, and moved toward more comprehensive development. When I was allowed to choose a team, I worked with committed professionals. We set "stretch" goals with clients, and those goals made the task more exciting and the team

[5] The Bank remains an attractive employer, offering relatively generous salaries and security, possibly leading to "golden cage" situations. However, the focus of this book is on the Bank as an international aid organization, created in the service of global development.

more committed. The Bank team co-innovated with often-overlooked talented country counterparts.

I also co-learned and co-innovated with many talented colleagues in developing countries. And I gained the enduring appreciation and loyalty of my Bank team—in a competitive institutional environment that did not always support such relationships. When empowered, I was able to break through the bureaucracy and to reconcile the recurring tensions between serving the Bank and the client country. It made an enormous difference to my effectiveness and country results when I was empowered and given adequate autonomy to co-create with clients.

I was attracted to high-risk/high-reward projects that had potentially transformative payoffs in terms of development outcomes. I lived through setbacks and challenges and learned to convert adversities into opportunities, proving that breakthroughs and innovation were possible—even if they unfolded at a slower pace than expected from a premier development institution.

In sum, my work on pursuing shared prosperity through digital transformation has been a journey of exploration, learning, fulfillment, and growth, and at times, fear and frustration, bordering on cynicism. It was often difficult to live up to my ideals and values, and to remain responsive to the urgent needs of client countries, even while engaging with unrepresentative governments and working within the constraints of the risk-averse global aid agencies. I learned to learn. Hopefully, I also empowered my clients to explore and innovate. I could sense the enthusiasm of clients, particularly the reformers and disempowered, as they feel they can be in control, and discover that the Bank is not a distant and powerful bureaucracy—but with staff who can be empathetic and open to co-learning.

After leaving the Bank, I have continued to advocate for accelerating digital transformation by partnering with other stakeholders and contributing to executive education for digital leaders. I have learned a lot from teaching and coaching younger colleagues attracted to new ideas and the latest technologies. Even if at times they underestimated the challenges of implementing their ideas, they have helped me test the waters and keep my knowledge fresh. Junior colleagues often lack guidance from their managers consumed by bureaucratic politics.

For the Bank and other aid agencies, my experience offers a challenge: will they find a way to leapfrog in their institutional reforms so they can truly realize the ongoing opportunity of the digital revolution? Will they find a way to truly listen to, learn from, and partner with in-country beneficiaries and counterparts? Will they find a way to empower employees to innovate and take responsible risks, be less absorbed with career politics and personal advancement, and more concerned with in-country effectiveness and results?

For development practitioners, this book is a report from the frontline, authored by a participant-observant of the development process. It offers an inquiry into the future of development assistance. Will they dare to break out of the comfort of disciplinary and sectoral silos to address the digital transformation process more holistically?

CHAPTER 3

Early Engagements

Abstract This chapter covers the Bank's development assistance in Indonesia and Palestine-Israel that helped the author appreciate the demand side of information technologies. Appointments in the Bank's corporate strategy and performance evaluation functions helped the author understand the inner workings of complex aid organizations like the Bank. He critiques the managerial culture of the Bank and its impact on innovation and risk taking as required to harness the digital revolution for development. He argues for a new style of development assistance that empowers client countries and engender ownership and innovation. He calls for a shift in strategic planning practice from rigid documentation and routine transactions to strategic thinking and agile, adaptive, learning, and communication-intensive processes.

Keywords Development assistance · Sudan · Indonesia · Palestine-Israel · Corporate strategy · Managerial culture

The Sudan Experience

I developed a fascination with the way technical assistance to developing countries can use data-intensive models as tools for policy analysis, investment planning, knowledge management, and institutional learning.

N. K. Hanna, *Economic Development in the Digital Age*,
https://doi.org/10.1007/978-3-031-54569-6_3

As a graduate student I examined the technical assistance provided to Sudan over 20 years. This technical assistance, funded by USAID and others, amounted to tens of millions of dollars and was delivered by famous and expensive consulting firms. Those were the days (early 1970s) when planners put much faith in quantitative models. These complex models inspired awe and empowered the experts and planners vis a vis the local policy makers and beneficiaries. These data-intensive models sprang not only from advances in econometrics, but also new computing and software languages that permitted the optimization and simulation of complex systems with multiple feedbacks. Much of the data needed to calibrate and validate these models had to be collected as part of technical assistance as there were no local information systems to regularly capture and use these data.

In the Sudan, I realized how information poverty limited the choices for all actors in development—planners, managers, investors, producers, and policy makers. It reinforced dependency. It penalized poor consumers and small producers even more. The planning models employed did not produce the desired results of developing local capacity, and empowering local stakeholders. The transfer of intangible technologies, like tangible ones, depended on complementary factors such as enabling policies and skills to make knowledge and innovation work for development.

My work in the Sudan led to the opportunity to testify to the US Congress on the potential for using satellite technologies to share knowledge and technology with developing countries.[1] These were pre-Internet days, and yet there was much hope that knowledge and technology "transfer" could quickly impact global development. Much of attention then, as it is now, was focused on the power of new technologies, regardless of institutional context and complementary local skills. Dealing with these issues was going to become central to my long career at the Bank which I joined as a Young Professional in 1975 after a well-attended farewell dancing party at the International House. I was eager and ready to dedicate myself to addressing humanity's key challenges.

I believed that the key to professional effectiveness was to be client-centered—defining the problem and seeking the solution jointly with the client (Argyris and Schon 1974). At times, this meant putting the interests of the client above the need to maintain team harmony and abide to

[1] Hearings before US House of Representatives, International Science and Technology Transfer Act of 1974.

the bureaucratic status quo. It also often meant focusing on innovative tasks that could open up new possibilities for my development practice, even if it challenged the dominant way of doing business and risked my career. By doing so, I may have underestimated the strength of bureaucratic inertia and resistance to change and not given sufficient attention to understanding the caution and fears of my peers and managers, and the need to patiently invest in building coalitions for innovation and reform. Winning support for innovation in a hierarchical and risk-averse organization requires significant personal and team investment.

Development Management in Indonesia

My first assignments as YP (1975–1976) were in urban and rural development. I visited urban slums in Jakarta where tropical rains were flooding poor neighborhoods and homes, saw children playing in the overflowing sewage, and then returned to my hotel emotionally exhausted. Much of the realities of the slums were out of sight of the Bank and IMF staff, often hidden from view by advertising boards for new boulevards and hotels.

I later visited the rural areas of Java while working on an irrigation and area development project. I saw beautiful rice terraces and lush green valleys and forests often concealing destitute and poor rural communities. In preparing an issues paper for a decision meeting on a project—where the project team would seek guidance on resolving key issues—I was instructed by my manager not to include issues for which we did not have ready answers. I began to learn what was permissible and what was counter to a risk-averse culture at the Bank. We were expected to have the answers to all the problems we acknowledge! We should have all the answers before presenting the project to the Bank's Executive Board. By project completion, all development problems would be solved!

During my visit to Jakarta I also met with some Bank staff who were seasoned experts in their fields. These staff often came from past colonial administrations. They had a long-term and holistic (ecosystem) view of development, informed by their long experience on the ground, even if they wrongly thought they had all the answers. Their views were in contrast to the relatively young and ambitious, former YP managers, who often relied on "off-the shelf" technocratic textbook solutions.

I fell in love with the natural beauty of Indonesia, and the rich artistic culture of Java and Bali. The lush green of tropical plants and forests often covered the underlying economic poverty in both urban and rural areas.

My early operational experience at the Bank (1976–1984) focused on Indonesia both at headquarters and at the resident mission in Jakarta. I covered several sectors: public and business management development; private sector development; science, technology, and innovation (STI); technical education; and institutional development, among others. As a hybrid country (loan) officer and economist, I tried to put investment operations in the broader context of sector policies and country assistance strategies.

Early on as a loan officer, I was expected to chair negotiations between the Bank and the Government of Indonesia for each proposed project. Bank delegation included relatively young sector specialists, lawyers, and procurement and finance specialists. Country counterparts included the most senior and experienced managers of the national planning agency, Ministry of Finance. The Ministry of Finance was then represented by Sri Mulyani, who later became the Indonesian Minister of Finance, and the Managing Director of the World Bank. The country delegation also included senior managers and heads of the concerned implementing ministries. Often these negotiations were carried out in Washington, with the Bank team having access to senior management and specialists to call upon, while the country team must consult with their government agencies remotely and were pressed to conclude the negotiations successfully and in relatively short time. I did my best to understand client's specific situation, rather than pressing for standard Bank positions. But I realized how easy for me and relatively-inexperienced negotiating Bank staff to come across as arrogant and at times misinformed of the country context and political economy. Often, I felt the Bank's bargaining power was not matched by its staff experience.

On invitation from Stanley Please, the country director, I decided to relocate to Jakarta and be close to the client. The assignment at the Resident Staff in Indonesia (RSI) was considered a privilege since Indonesia was perhaps the largest Bank borrower, enjoyed McNamara's special attention, and its resident mission had a level of autonomy that was exceptional for a centralized Bank. Bernie Bell, former director of RSI, and subsequently the regional VP for East Asia had exceptional skills in development diplomacy and enjoyed the trust of the local technocrats—who were educated in economics at UC Berkeley and trusted by the military and aid agencies. In chairing negotiations on several loans with the Indonesian delegations, I had earned the trust of my counterparts. Despite my junior level, the new country director wanted me to build on this trust and contribute to improving this critical client relationship.

On the way to Jakarta, my wife and I traveled through London, Amsterdam, Vienna, Greece, Egypt, and Thailand. We soaked up diverse cultures and civilizations. While traveling, I was reading Geertz's book on the religions of Java, and how the Indonesian culture was open and capable of synthesizing Islam, Christianity, and indigenous beliefs. I wanted to appreciate the art, history, institutions, social norms, and culture of this large and diverse nation. Geertz's pioneering work on the power of culture was a helpful guide.

While still at hotel Borobudur awaiting relocation to a house in Jakarta, I went on a first mission to the Outer Islands for a proposed regional development project. Upon return I received a confidential memo announcing the arrival of a VIP that I was expected to guide. That was my wife's way of getting my immediate attention to the arrival of our son, letting me know she was pregnant—life-changing news. Our rich cultural and social life would be affected by the medical and other challenges of raising a child in a developing country.

A few months later the new director had burn-out and returned to Washington. The relationship between the new regional VP for East Asia and Indonesia's key policy makers was frail. The VP had moved from the Africa region, where the Bank often dictated policy reforms, to the East Asia region, where major country clients enjoyed stronger voice and autonomy. Indonesia insisted on being treated as a development partner, and the country technocrats rightly felt they were as qualified as Bank experts. In devising economic policies, Senior Minister Wijojo had to navigate the complex relationship between the technocratic team at the central planning authority and the governing military. The central planning and policy making institution was not sufficiently developed. Minister Wijojo and his "Berkley mafia" economists preferred to rely on personalized relationships and trust in dealing with the Bank and other donors. The Bank's outgoing VP, Bernie Bell, enjoyed such trust as he invested much time listening and coaching the Indonesian team. The new RSI director faced the untenable task of turning around a deteriorating country relationship, even while placating the new VP, who was distrustful of the old Bank team and personal relationships, and a believer in the Bank's economic orthodoxy.

An example of this economic policy dialogue, or lack thereof, was the major report Indonesia's industrial and trade policies delivered during this managerial transition. The report offered a devastating critique of Indonesian technocrats' policies. Much of that critique could just as well be applied to the industrial policies pursued by other East Asian countries. Regardless of the merits of the several-volume report, it was presented with little dialogue and much arrogance. I got the sense that the authors were trying to prove their superior analytical skills and economic orthodoxy without any attempt to persuade or to adapt policy prescriptions to country conditions and the local policy development process. The immediate result was a breakdown of all communications. It took years to repair the damage, with a new resident director capable of managing his Bank superiors and working with key technocrats to jointly design and support policy solutions.

While navigating the complex development process at RSI, I observed day-to-day policy making and country assistance strategy in action, and grew to appreciate the central role of institutional and technological change in development. The Bank was dealing primarily with apex institutions ranging from the central bank and ministry of finance to the national planning authority and the national authorities for irrigation, highways, etc. To advance the transfer of resources and increase the Bank's leverage in policy reform, the new director aimed to consolidate multiple lending operations into fewer large ones. This shift fitted well with the Bank's corporate objectives, but reinforced the Indonesian government's tendency toward centralization, and reduced the opportunities to understand the problems of frontline implementation and to seek and incorporate bottom-up innovation and grassroots institutions. It also eliminated the need to have experienced technical staff on board at the RSI to help provide "hands-on" technical assistance and the transfer of tacit knowledge and project management expertise. Much needed but lacking was long-term systemic change linked to on-the-ground experience to secure sustainable results.

Public sector information systems were designed to move information up to the center, but gave little feedback to support implementation and left little room for local problem solving and learning. There was little horizontal flow of information within and across ministries. Cabinet meetings often benefited from timely information and scenarios that were developed within RSI, but RSI models and tools were not shared with or built within their ministries. The chief country economist admitted to me that sharing the models would uncover weaknesses in the Bank's data and assumptions and consequently undermine the Bank's scenarios and ability to persuade the Indonesian counterparts. I was concerned that our unquestioned assumptions may prove wrong, and the process of capacity building would be further undermined. Since, I observed how the lack of timely and reliable information was limiting choices and learning at all levels of government and for all actors in development, including business and NGOs.

I also observed how modern information systems can improve public expenditure and project management, demonstrated even during those early days of computerization in Indonesia (while I was in Indonesia, 1979–1983). I worked with the Ministry of Public Works, to cover these systems for roads, irrigation, and urban development programs. They amounted to more than half of the Bank's lending to Indonesia. Modernizing these systems led to much faster design and implementation of these programs, together with improved project and financial management, adaptation, monitoring, evaluation, and accountability. With faster communication, implementation, and disbursements, carry-over funds for annually approved projects were cut by half or more.

Indonesia presented major issues and choices for decentralization of development programs in view of its widespread spatial and cultural diversity and highly uneven development within and outside Java Island.[2] Development projects were distributed over many islands with a wider span than that of the US. I was concerned that Bank-funded projects and policy dialogue may be reinforcing centralized planning and institutions. The Bank was dedicating substantial funding to programs for irrigation, highways, electricity and other infrastructures, and the apex authorities that manage their sectoral policies and investments. Financing these programs fit well with the Bank's organizational structure and lending targets. So I devoted my attention to devise projects and programs to balance these centralizing forces via local district development, rural roads, and integrated area development for poor regions such as Jogjakarta rural development, among others. The challenge was to develop institutional setups that devolve and strengthen management, institutions, and finance to the local level, and yet engage the

[2] Indonesia is composed of 3000 inhabited islands, with total population of about 280 million (in 2022). Java, with a population of 150 million, is the world's most populous island.

central technical ministries in building capacity of their local counterparts to progressively integrate and manage their own local development programs. An equal challenge was to get the Bank to engage with lower levels of government and planning institutions, and to build its knowledge of, and partnerships with grassroots institutions.

I observed first-hand how the Bank was scorned as a technical assistance and knowledge transfer agency, despite its stores of data and publications. This was for several reasons. First of all, technical assistance (TA) loans/credits or TA components of investment projects were primarily used to prepare projects for Bank lending, and/or to supplement Bank staff implementation support of investment projects. Even when investment projects included tools for building local capacity and institutions, the share of TA funds and implementation support devoted to these long-term objectives was marginal.

Second, incentives for disbursing Bank loans far outweighed the more human resources-intensive capacity building and knowledge transfer activities. Similarly, incentives for conducting Bank-driven studies to design policy loans often displaced activities to support government-owned policy studies and local think tanks. Incentives for Bank staff may have unintentionally led to perpetuating dependency rather than facilitating local capacity building, or what has been recently termed "localization" in the aid jargon.

Third, many borrowers of Bank loans were reluctant to pay for what they could not see and touch—the intangibles promised by TA loans or components of hardware-dominated investments. Borrower's reluctance was often reinforced by the disparities in compensation between their own public servants and borrower-funded international consultants. Frequently, the Bank made its funding for major investment and policy loans conditional on the borrower's acceptance of funding TA and high-cost international consultants. This did not engender ownership of TA loans.

Fourth, the Bank did not prioritize its TA and technology transfer roles. It did not develop the staffing and special skills that are attuned to practical solutions during implementation. Perhaps it was assumed the Bank would collaborate with specialized UN agencies who would have more of the technical skills to lead technology transfer activities. In reality, the Bank played the role of a technology transfer agency only within the context of investment and policy lending. Technology transfer, however, does not end with buying hardware and off-the-shelf solutions—it requires substantial adaptation, experimentation, learning, and complementary policy and institutional measures. In today's world, digital technology transfer calls for investment in digital transformation as a socio-technical process. In a digitally-driven changing world, the lack of capacity and experience in technology transfer cripples the Bank's role as a technology transfer agent.

Finally, the Bank has yet to address the challenges involved in moving its development advisory services from imposed blueprints to tools for empowerment and learning.[3] The Bank has been increasing its investment in analytical and advisory services. It faces a fundamental choice: invest in its diagnostic tools to reinforce due diligence and independent assessment of the countries policies and institutions, or invest in new tools and modalities that allow for joint and participatory diagnosis and problem solving with its clients. While incentives within the Bank may favor the former option, sustainable development effectiveness is likely to favor the latter.

On request from the Planning Agency in Indonesia, I did a review of the TA embedded in Bank investment lending to Indonesia over two decades (1970–1990). The Agency had complained that the Bank-funded TA amounted to 20% of its investment portfolio. This share seemed to be constant or increasing despite the promise that such TA funding would decline as Indonesia built its own staffing and local capacity to carry out these activities. Upon examining this volume of TA lending, the largest among all Bank borrowers at the time, it became clear that most of this TA was targeted to facilitate the preparation and implementation of Bank-funded projects to meet the quality requirements of the Bank itself. At the time, there was no attempt to address the underlying local civil service policies and practices to identify the capacity gap. Bank staff and managers were mired in old-fashioned lending processes. Indonesia was the biggest Bank borrower and a model for others to follow.

At the time (1970s–1980s), the Indonesian government was flush with revenues from oil exports, but suffered from a severe shortage of qualified and experienced managers and institutional leadership. The shortage was evident since Indonesia's independence, but educational institutions were slow to respond to this gap. Paternalism, top-down centralized decision-making, and underdeveloped management development systems

[3] See Hanna, 2002. "Development Advisory Services: From Blueprints to Learning" in *Making Development Work*, pp. 135–158.

within public institutions exacerbated this shortage and led to leakage of resources, corruption, and project implementation problems.

At the request of the Minister for administrative reform, I led a multi-donor study to create a national strategy for management development. The resident mission director was cautiously supportive of the study. No additional budget was allocated for it from the Bank to carry out the study, apart from adding this challenging task to my work as country officer. I mobilized staff and trust funds via USAID, the Ford and Rockefeller Foundations, ILO, and French aid. The study covered current policies, needs, and sources for education, training, and development of public and business managers. I also had the opportunity to travel and meet leaders of management education and development institutions, such as the Indian Institute of Management, the Asian Institute of Management in Manila, and leading institutions in Japan, the UK, the US, and France.

The Bank's mainstream economists were skeptical of management as a discipline. They were often promoted to higher levels of management based on their technical and communications skills as well as their overall fit with the Bank's managerial culture. Until 1985, there was no Bank department or global practice for institutional development, public administration, public sector management, or governance.

There was no tradition of professional management in Indonesia, particularly in the public sector. Managers were selected primarily based on their technical expertise and personal connections. Management education focused mainly on applied economics or traditional public administration. There were no managerial development programs within public or business institutions.

When we completed our three-volume study outlining the proposed national management development strategy, and major policies, institutional and educational reforms, the regional chief economist, a trade economist by education, objected to its publication citing the Bank's lack of demonstrated success and specialized staff in civil service policies and public sector management. To him, management and institutional development did not qualify as formal economic and sectoral work. Despite internal resistance from senior Bank economists, the Indonesian government and other development partners insisted on its publication.

The Bank's program director then tried to use the demonstrated demand for Bank work in this new area to create a unit to focus on development management. After a no go from the Asia VP, this unit was later created in the Africa Region when the program director was promoted to Africa's VP. By the time the Bank accepted management and institutional development as a legitimate assistance target, I had already moved to the Bank's newly created corporate strategy unit.

Working for Peace in the Middle East

In late 1994, I got another challenging assignment as a lead economist/ country officer in the newly established Resident Mission in Jerusalem. The Oslo Accords for peace between Israel and Palestine (West Bank and Gaza) have just been signed, and the US, the EU, and the Bank's President Wolfensohn were committed to help both parties make peace through a secure Israel and a viable Palestinian state. This two-year engagement is too complex and important to cover briefly in a memoir about the role of digital technologies in development, so I will only discuss its relevance to the opportunities arising from the demand for digital solutions.[4]

The assignment was even more challenging than I expected. It was a perfect fit with my background and my desire for peace in the Middle East. I saw the devastating economic impact of war as I grew up in Egypt during two wars with Israel (1956 and 1967) and a proxy war with Saudi Arabia in Yemen. At school, I learned about the evils of Western imperialism and the Israeli occupation and dispossession of Palestinian lands. At the same time, I also empathized with the Israelis who were discriminated against in the West and went through the horrors of the Holocaust—I knew what it was like to suffer discrimination growing up as a Christian in a Muslim country. I thought I could effectively relate to all parties and, as a US citizen, I could use the US government influence to promote regional peace and shared prosperity. I shared Shimon Perez's vision of the "New Middle East" and hoped to make a difference by building bridges for peace.

In preparation, I read a lot about the political and economic situation in the West bank and Gaza. My wife hosted groups of university professors, NGO leaders, and Bank colleagues to debate the future of

[4] I hope to devote a separate memoir on my experience in development assistance in Indonesia and Palestine-Israel, and perhaps corporate strategy at the Bank. The main focus here is on how these experiences and lessons have shaped my approach to digital transformation.

the Middle East and my pending departure to Jerusalem. The Old City of Jerusalem awakened passion and nostalgia. The intifada invoked dread and hope. As a colleague from an NGO told me: "Every act you take while living in Jerusalem is a political one, including who you buy your bread from!"

We flew to Jerusalem on the eve of 1995. The taxi driver took an unlit West Bank road from Tel Aviv to East Jerusalem. My 14-year-old son was worried about his new life away from his friends and about starting a new school in the middle of the school year. The dark road to East Jerusalem added to his misery. He cried himself to sleep.

At the American Colony Hotel, the three of us settled into a small room. The hotel was in a beautiful setting in the heart of the ancient city. We visited the Old City where even the stones could heal. The smells of falafel, shawarma, kunafa, and Arabic coffee took me straight back to my childhood in Alexandria. So did the music and songs of Umm Kulthum enveloping the winding narrow streets.

Getting settled in East Jerusalem was a challenge: navigating local bureaucracy to access phone service, purchase a car, buy essential appliances—everything had to be bought from a single authorized dealer in Tel Aviv (minus exorbitant Israeli taxes) and delivered under Israeli army surveillance. We also had to move the furniture we were able to buy through many check points on the way from Gaza and the West Bank on to Israel and to East Jerusalem. Buying a car involved many hurdles and several months of waiting. The Bank's newly established office operated from a building basement—until it was properly set up outside of Jerusalem. The office had to deal with similar challenges and offered no help.

After several months without access to communications and transportation, crammed between unpacked boxes from Washington and with no family or friends, even my savvy New Yorker wife was about to give up! I offered little comfort as I had to travel throughout Gaza and the West Bank, responding to continuous emergencies while in the process of initiating a new assistance program and setting up new institutions. To make matters worse, in the absence of a fully functional office, my wife often had to facilitate the visiting missions from Washington. Luckily, a group of Palestinian families soon befriended my wife, practically adopting her, and we started to have a social life again—closures permitting. Early frustrations gave way to rich social interactions. As many who cope in times of turbulence and uncertainty, Palestinians invested in social capital and resilient communities, and lived from one day to the next. The past was traumatic. The future was uncertain.

These were uncertain times ridden with fear and insecurity. There were bus explosions, night army raids, helicopter surveillance often followed by house demolitions—right in our middle-class neighborhood in East Jerusalem.[5] Unpredictable closures of main routes were frequent. When closures were suddenly imposed, my son guided the International School bus driver to reach the school in West Jerusalem. We were warned that in case of local skirmishes, the teenage children of UN and other international staff might be beaten by Israeli soldiers and imprisoned without embassy notification. We had to get the UNDP staff to urgently issue an international ID card for our son as a protection measure.

Despite a prevailing sense of disempowerment around us, we were still privileged people living in a privileged part of East Jerusalem and enjoying relative security as US citizens. My wife and son were able to quickly learn some Arabic and Hebrew. We struck friendships with the pro-peace members of both societies. When inviting Israelis to our dinner table together with Palestinians and US consulate staff, we would pick them up from West Jerusalem to allay their fears of coming to East Jerusalem—a part of town with an Arab majority. Still we enjoyed the multicultural setting and the lively discussions in a charged political environment, and we felt dedicated to the peace cause that brought us there in the first place.

The Oslo Peace Process brought about much hope and uncertainty, and the process of land and border separation was expected to progress through painful negotiations, with US and EU political and financial support. There was widespread popular support for the "two-state solution", epitomized in the Nobel Peace Prize award to Arafat, Rabin, and Perez. But the process was challenged by growing Israeli settlements and the radicals on both sides.

On November 4, 1995, we were at a party at the US consulate when we heard the sad news of Rabin's assassination. The Prime Minister of Israel was assassinated while speaking at a rally in support of the Oslo Accords. The attack was carried out by a radical Jewish law student and was meant to halt the peace process. Although we were used to daily

[5] Upon return to Washington we experienced mild symptoms of Post-Traumatic Stress Disorder (PTSD) triggered by the sound of hovering helicopters.

dramatic events, this was by far the most consequential one for peace in the Middle East.

My primary focus in Jerusalem was to help build economic cooperation between Palestinian and Israeli businesses to generate employment and attract investment in the Palestinian territories. I thought economic progress and hope for the future would build a political basis for just peace. I hoped to facilitate this through a series of industrial technology parks on the promised border between Israel and Palestine, and thus contribute to shared prosperity. This corridor of industrial development was also expected to reduce dependence on Palestinian laborers crossing the border daily and create access to new and secure jobs.

This vision was not easy to sell to two deeply traumatized peoples. On the Israeli side, the Ministry of Industry wanted to have the industrial estate straddle both sides of the border between Israel and Gaza for a variety of reasons, including maintaining control over at least an equal part of the estate while having access to offsite and onsite facilities. The Palestinians and the donors preferred to have a jointly secured estate on the Palestinian side of the Border. The Palestinians saw this also as a symbol of their autonomy and yearning for independence. I visited some Israeli industrial estates, including one on the border with Gaza controlled by the Israeli army, with Gazan labor in Israeli-owned factories. To address the Palestinian desire for autonomy and hopefully independence, I wanted to engage Israeli expertise and security in the project without agreeing to Israel's unilateral control.

When I proposed this to the Palestinian Minister of Industry in Gaza, he was skeptical that Israel would "let go" and deliver on promises for closure-free movement to and from the estate.[6] At the time, I shared the assurances and promises from various donor staff, particularly from the US and the EU. I encouraged the minister to set his doubts aside and prioritize the establishment of an autonomous authority for regulating and investing in the proposed estate. I had faith in the promises and the

[6] His doubts were caused by a long chain of disappointments. He had lived in the diaspora for a generation, with members of his family living in Jordan, Kuwait, Lebanon, and Egypt, among others. But he did not lose hope for independence.

broad support of the international community.[7] He gradually became an avid supporter of this venture. It was a leap of faith in the power of the peace constituency after decades of disappointments.

The vision attracted increasing support from the US, the EU, Jewish Americans, Israeli businesses and investors, as well as the Palestinian diaspora in the US, Latin America, Jordan, and the rest of the Middle East. Working with Professor Boyson of the University of Maryland, and Gershon Baskin, CEO of IPCRI, an Israeli-Arab NGO, we surveyed potential investors to determine the preconditions and incentives needed for investment in these technology parks. The interest in joint business investments and sustainable solutions was very high, provided security and the free movement of labor, goods, and services were guaranteed. Serviced land and physical infrastructure for industry were in short supply and prohibitively expensive, yet, labor-intensive, export-oriented industrial production could create sustainable employment and stimulate economic growth, starting with Gaza.

An early example of US political support was the US Senate resolution sent to President Bill Clinton in support of the border industrial estates vision. The US, an ardent supporter of Israel and a peace mediator, felt these border estates would provide employment and economic opportunities for Palestinians while ensuring Israel's security. Staggering unemployment, deepening poverty, and increasing despair were leading to terrorism and border closures. This motivated me to stay committed to a risky initiative despite doubts on the part of some senior Bank managers.

I worked with all parties on the realization of this vision. They included the USAID, the US embassy in Tel Aviv and the Consulate in East Jerusalem, the Palestine Development and Investment Company (PADICO), the Israeli Foreign Ministry, Palestinian ministries of Industry, Trade and Finance, the European Union representative, the UN special coordinator, and various Israeli and Palestinian business leaders. I viewed this as a process of building bridges and trust to create the right environment for private investment and provide a model for joint ventures across borders. We worked against ambitious targets and fleeting hope.

[7] In the US, the State Department and the Congress were strong supports of the border estate program as a vehicle for peace and security for Israel, and employment and prosperity for the Palestinians. The Palestine Development and Investment Company (PADICO) was willing to invest in onsite development on behalf of the PA.

Bank management was anxious to get the infrastructure investment in place and viewed the first industrial park at the main border entry to Gaza as an easy entry point to a long-term program. Unfortunately, the prospects were dimmed by the election of Netanyahu as Prime Minister in 1996 and the rising influence of the settlers and right-wing extremists. I invited Israeli security staff, including the former Israeli military governor of the West Bank, to assess security requirements and the latest technological solutions to address them. The US agreed to provide guarantees and finances for such security-enhancing solutions. Pressure was high to demonstrate some signs of progress to save the peace "process".

The Bank proceeded with infrastructure investments including telecommunications, roads, water and sewage treatment plants and incubators without awaiting the necessary guarantees from Israel to secure free movement to and from the park. I objected to Bank management proceeding without such guarantees as they were essential to the viability of private investments of prospective park tenants. I chose to play a long game, to create badly needed employment for Palestinians and secure environment for investors. But Bank management could not wait for Israeli guarantees or press for long-term solutions. I attempted to "do good" by pursuing a risky program to create jobs in support of a shared vision of two-state solution. I almost lost my job and career at the Bank.

My last month in Jerusalem—before I left for a new assignment in Washington, DC—was a mix of sorrow and celebration. We were invited to farewell parties and dinners hosted by the public Palestinian Authority (PA) and private (PADICO) sectors, donor agencies (USAID, EU), Bank colleagues, the Israeli Ministry of Foreign Affairs, and friends—even the Bank's security guards. Many were anxious about the fate of the border estates program. For us, it was a very emotional good-bye. I was also invited to celebrate the Palestinian "independence" day in Gaza where Arafat presented me with a medal of honor. Martin Indyk, US ambassador to Israel, ambassadors of other donor countries, USAID, and Terry Larson, UN regional coordinator, were all there.

In my last meeting before I left the Jerusalem mission, Shimon Perez promised he would press for progress on negotiations once his government won the election in a few days. With his party's loss soon thereafter, the prospects for the first border industrial park diminished.

The Bank proceeded with the project without the necessary "closure-proof" guarantees. Management was keen to demonstrate results on the ground. I felt that proceeding with physical investments before securing both parties' ownership of the enabling policy and security environments was risky. Nevertheless, the project was approved by the Bank and co-financed with other donors. It got the Bank's innovation award. I took the risks of initiating a pioneering project and did most of the heavy lifting to help my Palestinian counterparts prepare the project. But I was holding out for Israeli guarantees for free movement from and to the industrial park. These guarantees were essential for the viability of export-oriented industries. Subsequently, frequent border closures blocked the movement of goods and services. Israel bombarded Gaza and destroyed much of the infrastructure that was built, including infrastructure financed by donor and private sector investors. A rare window of opportunity to build business partnerships and infrastructures for peace and economic empowerment was closing. The settlers were gaining ground and establishing facts on the ground.[8]

In light of the growing restrictions on cross-border movements, the idea of "virtual" collaboration among young Israelis and Palestinians in software development was gaining some popularity. No cross-border movement would be required yet educated and skilled young people on both sides could engage in high-value collaboration. Israel, "the startup nation", would have much to offer (and business gains to share from) a peaceful neighborhood. Although virtual collaboration would not address all the pressing needs and aspirations of most young and resentful Palestinians, it would perhaps alleviate the rising despair within the Palestinian territories and offer a new model for cooperation for peace and shared prosperity.

With the rise of extremism, technology-assisted doomsday scenarios are becoming more likely. Israel and many other countries are constantly improving their surveillance tools. Israel has a cutting-edge cybersecurity industry. Israeli leaders may be tempted to create a total surveillance regime in the West Bank. Already today, whenever Palestinians make a phone call, post something on Facebook, or travel from one city to another, they are likely to be monitored. The data are then analyzed with the aid of big data algorithms, ensuring total control over 2.5 million West Bank Palestinians.[9]

[8] In hindsight, some may argue that Israel would not have abided by the "closure free" guarantees in a rapidly deteriorating political environment, with the rise of the political right in Israel and Hamas in Gaza.

[9] Yuval Harari (2019).

Was I too optimistic about a technical solution to the Arab–Israeli conflict? Did the Israeli labor government underestimate the power of the settlers and the rise of the extreme right, and thus squandered the narrow window of opportunity of negotiating the conditions for viable border industrial estates? Did I ignore the cancer of occupation and daily humiliation and disempowerment, in the hope for breaking a continuing economic siege and building bridges for peace? Did the UN, the Bank, and aid agencies overpromise by asking the Palestinians to put their faith in a long process toward peace with dignity?

Can we have economic development without peace—with the Palestinian economy remaining under siege? Alternatively, can we have peace without development—with a high level of youth unemployment and apartheid-like conditions? Would a vision of shared prosperity, driven by Israel's digital technology innovation, Arab petrodollars, educated youth, and hard-working Palestinian labor help overcome past grievances and become inclusive of the Palestinians? I often wondered. I suffered many sleepless nights.

Moral leadership is needed, as digital technologies can be tools for war or peace. I believe leadership on both sides missed a major opportunity for a peaceful and prosperous Middle East. As I had to leave Jerusalem for a new assignment in corporate strategy of the Bank under Wolfensohn, I left with many hopes and dreams unrealized. I still hope both sides can overcome extremist factions and build on a new, just, and inclusive vision for the region—choosing peace over terror and apartheid. There is a lot of good will, pro-peace civil society organizations, and potential support from international organizations to find win–win solutions for peace and prosperity. But major opportunities for peace and development do not come so often.

I did not expect that developing viable industrial states at the border between Israel and Palestine could substitute for political freedom and the development of an independent Palestinian state. It was hoped that such cooperative investment in peace and economic development would build mutual trust and provide incremental steps toward sustainable development and security for both peoples. However, the recent Israel-Gaza war (started October 7, 2023) made it much harder to envision such solutions. It made clear that temporary measures to alleviate Palestinian suffering and return to the status quo would fall far short of addressing the main problems of occupation and disempowerment.

Country Engagements Takeaways

Long country engagements—living and working in resident missions in Indonesia and Palestine—taught me the importance of a deeper understanding of country context, political economy, leadership institutions, and potential paths to development. I really understood that country specificity or "one-size does not fit all" is a demanding practice requiring long-term involvement in institutional and technological transformations. Country ownership of reforms, stakeholder participation and empowerment, and continuous evaluation and learning are all essential ingredients of sustained and inclusive development.

Resident mission assignments offered me and my family rare multicultural social lives. In the field, the Bank is just one among many bilateral and multilateral aid agencies, UN organizations, global non-governmental institutions, and private foundations. Apart from the familiar aid agency employees, we made friends in local communities and enjoyed the company of their cultural and intellectual leaders. In Jerusalem, we had the unique fortune to engage the leaders of two societies (often in conflict), together with aid agency staff, in thoughtful conversation at our dinner table. These experiences helped my family to appreciate the importance of my development work. They led me to adopt a holistic view of the host country, its history, culture, art, and institutions. I also came to realize the potential of partnerships with other actors of the development community.

Learning is relational and contextual. I learned the most about development when I was on field missions, in close interaction with Bank teams and country clients. Field missions offered a close look at real development challenges and presented a learning environment free from the constraints of a centralized bureaucracy. Reduced hierarchy among mission team members, however temporary, as well as intense interaction with country stakeholders in the local context were key to agile learning.

My convictions, sense of urgency, and empathy for those I encountered during country engagements often led me to challenge the "status quo" and the Bank's institutional rigidities. Some colleagues saw me as idealistic or perhaps not willing to compromise in order to stay in line with Bank norms and imperatives. I tried my best to be a change agent, a loyal critic. Concerns about country ownership and stakeholder empowerment (acting as a hand-holder) often conflicted with Bank leverage and donor conditionalities (task master). Some influential Bank economists felt obliged to compete with IMF staff where conditionality was in vogue. They were rewarded for highly critical policy reviews of their country counterparts. These reviews were influenced by internal peer-review standards and often distorted conceptions of professional excellence and effectiveness, where the Bank is the sole definer of the problem and solution (Argyris and Schon 1974).

The understanding of client country conditions (as internally constructed and shared within the Bank's headquarters) was often considered more important than the country field reality.[10] Field-oriented staff who excelled in serving their clients were suspected of "going native" and the results they delivered were often ignored by Bank management. Maybe this disconnect was caused by the domination of large Western shareholders, as well as the gap between Bank staff, mainly recruited from elite US and UK universities, and the poor they were expected to serve. I wondered. My empathy with the client drove me to learn more about country conditions and to view the country as a whole. I hoped a more accurate understanding of reality would emerge when profiles were co-created with in-country counterparts.

My convictions informed my sense of purpose, strengthened my commitment and resilience, and helped me overcome many institutional hurdles. What can be more important than eradicating extreme poverty and building a better future for humankind, I thought! It was a privilege to serve from a relatively comfortable and secure position, so why not take some career risks!

It was in 2004 that Jim Wolfensohn, World Bank President, a demanding development practitioner and banker, while chairing a Board meeting on the e-Lanka project that I presented, complimented us by saying: "I have waited 10 long years to see such a ground- breaking digital transformation project"; and added "I hope to see much more of such thought leadership". It was clear that when empowered, given adequate autonomy and allowed to co-create with clients, we were able to break through the bureaucracy, reconcile the recurring tensions between serving the Bank and the client country, and deliver exceptional results. Yet the personal costs incurred by the pioneers were high. The mainstreaming of the e-Sri Lanka innovations within the Bank was slow mainly

[10] Bank staff have to manage two realities, one when they are on mission interacting with clients in the field, while the other is a socially-constructed reality (sanitized reports) for senior management and the Board.

due to turf conflicts, staff changes, misalignment across several managerial layers, and other institutional learning constraints. While such constraints are common across sectors and aid agencies, they tend to slow the pace of developmental learning and innovation at a time when the digital revolution and global development challenges are most pressing.

I often wondered if I was simply ahead of my time in pioneering digital transformation assistance at the Bank. Did I underestimate the personal risks and institutional constraints involved? Perhaps my zeal came across as too critical of the status quo. Perhaps I was a meddlesome intellectual gadfly in the eyes of more conservative managers. Maybe I was too impatient with the slow response of a large development bureaucracy. I tried to be a change agent and loyal critic.[11] After all, the Bank had substantial resources and talent, and often reacted to external criticism, albeit with some delay, as with adjustment lending and the impact of Bank-funded projects on the environment.

Are these words of despair? By no means! I loved the mission of development. I was fortunate to work for an influential organization with a mandate to fight global poverty. So far, the Bank proved indispensable during global financial crises, entered new fields of assistance, and moved toward more comprehensive development. When I was allowed to choose a team, I worked with committed professionals. We set "stretch" goals with clients, and those goals made the task more exciting and the team more committed. The Bank team co-innovated with often-overlooked talented country counterparts.

I also co-learned and co-innovated with many talented colleagues in developing countries. And I gained the enduring appreciation and loyalty of my Bank team—in a competitive institutional environment that did not always support such relationships. When empowered, I was able to break through the bureaucracy and to reconcile the recurring tensions between serving the Bank and the client country. It made an enormous difference to my effectiveness and country results when I was empowered and given adequate autonomy to co-create with clients.

I was attracted to high-risk/high-reward projects that had potentially transformative payoffs in terms of development outcomes. I lived through

[11] The Bank remains an attractive employer, offering relatively generous salaries and security, possibly leading to "golden cage" situations for some, particularly for non-US citizens. However, the focus of this book is on the Bank as an international aid organization, created in the service of global development.

setbacks and challenges and learned to convert adversities into opportunities, proving that breakthroughs and innovation were possible—even if they unfolded at a slower pace than expected from a premier development institution.

In sum, my work on pursuing shared prosperity through digital transformation has been a journey of exploration, learning, fulfillment, and growth, and at times, fear and frustration, bordering on cynicism. It was often difficult to live up to my ideals and values, and to remain responsive to the urgent needs of client countries, even while engaging with unrepresentative governments and working within the constraints of the risk-averse global aid agencies. I learned to learn. Hopefully, I also empowered my clients to explore and innovate. I could sense the enthusiasm of clients, particularly the reformers and disempowered, as they feel they can be in control, and discover that the Bank is not a distant and powerful bureaucracy—but with staff who can be empathetic and open to co-learning.

After leaving the Bank, I have continued to advocate for accelerating digital transformation by partnering with other stakeholders and contributing to executive education for digital leaders. I have learned a lot from teaching and coaching younger colleagues attracted to new ideas and the latest technologies. Even if at times they underestimated the challenges of implementing their ideas, they have helped me test the waters and keep my knowledge fresh. Junior colleagues often lack guidance from their managers consumed by bureaucratic politics.

For the Bank and other aid agencies, my experience offers a challenge: will they find a way to leapfrog in their institutional reforms so they can truly realize the ongoing opportunity of the digital revolution? Will they find a way to truly listen to, learn from, and partner with in-country beneficiaries and counterparts? I hope they find a way to empower employees to innovate and take responsible risks, be less absorbed with career politics and personal advancement, and more concerned with in-country effectiveness and results.

For development practitioners, this book is a report from the frontline, authored by a participant-observant of the development process. It offers an inquiry into the future of development assistance. Will they dare to break out of the comfort of disciplinary and sectoral silos to address the digital transformation process more holistically?

Reflecting back upon my various country experiences, I draw several key lessons:

- Country policy assistance demands diplomacy, empowerment, and ownership throughout the design and implementation process. Effective and sustainable Bank-country policy dialogue demands building trust and local policy institutions.
- The Bank has comparative advantages as convener, policy setter, and public investor. Yet, it faces many systemic constraints to its roles as agent of technical assistance, capacity building, and knowledge transfer.
- Developing leadership and professional public and business management cadres is a priority, particularly for new institutions and economic sectors like those responsible for digital transformation.
- Aid agencies' bias for short-termism, perhaps to act and demonstrate, should be balanced with a long-term view and incentives to build institutions and design for resilience and sustainability.
- Development professionals should listen carefully and modestly, then act with conviction and a sense of urgency.
- Peace and economic justice are essential to sustained development. Depending on stakeholders' values, digital technology can play a positive or negative role.

Strategic Planning and Evaluation

Shifting from the Bank's clients to its internal management, I served in a variety of corporate staff functions: corporate strategy and development effectiveness evaluation functions, I gained insights into how the Bank is strategically managed and what factors determine its development effectiveness. These insights are critical to understanding how the Bank responds to stakeholder's demands concerning digital transformation and other strategic, cross-cutting global challenges. Who elicits and elucidates tomorrow's questions? Who shapes and monitors the Bank's strategic behavior? In particular, how does corporate management respond to new dimensions of development such as digital transformation?

To learn about ongoing best practice in strategic planning and management, I led a team that interviewed the CEOs and/or chief strategy officers of about 90 major organizations, in public, business, and academic sectors. Based on this survey, I authored a first Bank published paper on strategic planning and management to guide the Bank's own newly established corporate strategy function (Hanna 1985).

Strategic planning has to shift from rigid documentation, data generation, and routine transactions to strategic thinking, data-analytics, and agile, adaptive and interactive processes. This conclusion flew in the face of the prevailing beliefs of those who established this new function at the Bank. The name chosen for this function was "Institution Planning Division" which implied developing long-range master plans. It was housed within the vice presidency of financial policy and planning, with a close link to corporate budgeting. The idea was to develop a systematic process to generate a central plan or a front-end framework to guide the Bank's annual budget allocation.

McNamara did not institutionalize strategic planning during his 13 years (1968–1981) at the helm. Instead, he was the de-facto chief strategist. He shaped the Bank as no one before him or since. The Bank that McNamara left in 1981 was unrecognizable to most development observers. It became a much larger and complex organization. Its membership had continued to expand into a global organization. The Bank began to address problems of income disparity and poverty. It entered sectors such as education and health, where progress was inevitably slow. It became deeply involved in the economic and social conditions of its borrowers. Throughout this journey, McNamara took a top-down approach to change management. He used his annual addresses to the Board of Governors at the Bank's Annual Meetings to set his strategic agenda and created new cadre of mangers via the YP program. He created new central departments to enter new fields such as urban and rural development, then systematically pushed for mainstreaming these new practices across regional operations.

Despite successes in his strategic management, McNamara left a major gap by not institutionalizing a strategic planning and management system. His Planning, Programming, and Budgeting System (PPBS) was heavy on programming and number crunching, but light on integrating strategic thinking and innovation into operations. Silos were created to deal with new initiatives. He alone could connect and drive these silos to deliver a coherent Bank response for a fast-changing global environment. This made the task of introducing strategic planning difficult after his retirement. The gap was most felt when Clausen took over the presidency of the Bank in 1981.

During 1984–1987, while I was trying to build a new corporate strategy function, under Clausen and Joe Wood, key senior managers considered corporate strategy as an aggregation of country assistance strategies (later called country partnership strategies) and programs. In turn, country assistance strategies were an aggregation of separate projects or 3-year lending programs. Others viewed strategic planning as an exercise in short-term forecasting, a front-end to the Bank's annual budgeting and resource allocation. Others yet believed that strategic planning was not applicable to a highly political organization with multiple stakeholders and global reach. Apart from prevailing misconceptions, strategic planning was kept hostage to a dysfunctional President Council where the two most senior VPs were at logger-heads to protect their turf. Corporate issues were often viewed through a zero-sum lens.

My own job and my colleagues' careers were at risk as we were part of the financial complex, yet needed to work with colleagues in Operations where most of the action (lending operations) occurs. We were therefore asked to keep our heads low, remain "invisible soldiers", and avoid analyzing controversial issues.

Most critical was the lack of ownership of the function on the part of President Clausen, and later Conable and the top members of his Management Council. I recall a meeting we had with the chief corporate strategist and several senior management members of General Electric (GE) to discuss best practices in corporate strategy and explore how to get our top management more involved, if not committed. Should we present them with challenging scenarios and topics for the future? Should we focus on crisis-like issues? The chief strategist thought our chances were slim in institutionalizing the strategic management function, as we were missing the most critical success factor: CEO ownership of the function. We were told strategic management has to start from the top. It should be the CEO's tool to manage strategically. We returned to our work dispirited.

Despite these challenges, we kept trying. For example, as the Secretariat of the Future Role of the Bank (FROB) we initiated a corporate planning exercise that engaged 200 seasoned staff and middle managers and addressed a wide range of cross-cutting issues, The FROB exercise was a major investment in strategic and analytical thinking that was rare among aid agencies. But in the end, only a small part of this intellectual investment was used.[12] The President's Management Council was not prepared to address many of the emerging strategic issues.

[12] But it led to the Bank's Executive Board approval of a general capital increase, and increased share of policy-based operations in overall Bank lending portfolio.

In considering the evolution of the Bank's business, we identified several strategic issues for management attention. For example, the need for appropriate incentives and aggressive redeployment of staff and budgetary resources away from mature businesses to more promising development areas of tomorrow, such as the digital economy, which require by nature high staff intensity and risk taking. It called for strengthening Bank foresight and strategic thinking capabilities at all levels of leadership to manage a growing number of uncertainties: financial, technological, and political. The identified agenda was shared with the task forces involved in the reorganization and was welcomed by a large number of middle managers. But it was not addressed at top management level.[13]

The strategic planning unit was lacking the authorizing environment needed to effect strategic change.[14] I was acting chief of the planning unit at the time. I saw the uncertain times for the planning function and the Bank as an opportunity to show how the function can add timely value to institutional renewal exercises. I advised the chair of the reorganization's steering group, Kim Jaycox, and advocated for creating a strong corporate strategic planning function to provide foresight and facilitate change management—and avoid dramatic reorganizations and episodic breakdowns. But there was no clear responsibility for implementing the reorganization, and for minimizing the human toll, country relationships breakdowns, and endemic institutional and cultural problems the reorganization would generate.

My team and I drew some scenarios of the changing mix of services that the Bank would provide and their implications for the skill mix and

[13] We also interviewed each member of the President's Council to help frame and reach consensus on strategic issues facing the Bank. The emerging strategic agenda was expected to be systematically discussed and managed among the stakeholders, via task forces, with accountabilities and time frames for resolving them. One memorable comment came from my interview with Ernie Stern, then SVP for Operations, who questioned whether it was at all possible to extend planning for lending programs beyond the one- or two-year horizon.

[14] I planned lunches with senior managers where I was both an advocate and a learner. I was also engaged with several staff networks advocating for institutional reform and renewal, such as the Staff Association, and the Values in Development group that were addressing the challenges Bank staff were facing when navigating between client development challenges and the Executive Board. Few reform-minded senior staff were contributing to an "underground press" urging reform in the pre-Internet age.

staffing over the mid-term horizon. This was at the rising peak of adjustment lending. Our analysis indicated that the immediate rise of policy and structural adjustment lending, up to a Board-established ceiling, will demand substantial rise in recruiting macroeconomists, and significant cut in technical staff. That change would taper off and then reverse over the medium term. I discussed the associated risks of depleting the technical project expertise, and costly changes in expertise and experience on board. The answer from a leading member of the steering group is that he hoped all staff would be macroeconomists, and sectoral expertise would not be needed any longer! The macroeconomists tribe won, at least for the short term! Human resource policies were not seriously considered.

I carried some of the lessons of my first assignment in strategic planning to my next round of corporate strategy and organizational change during 1996–1998, executed under the completely different leadership style of President Jim Wolfensohn. While I was nearing the end of my resident mission assignment in Jerusalem (1996), I was observing videos of the new President challenging his senior managers and calling for fundamental reforms of the Bank. As prospects for peace in Jerusalem were declining, I was attracted to join a small core team of staff to work on a new corporate strategy and corresponding budgetary reforms. I flew directly from Jerusalem to Washington to take a dream job and recoup my earlier learning investment in strategic planning.

This corporate strategy initiative was clearly driven from the top, by Wolfensohn, a President who was former owner and CEO of his boutique investment bank, and lacked the patience to deal with a large, slow changing professional services organization and with a resident Executive Board representing over 180 countries. Some of his most senior managers were alienated by his style of change management as he clearly wanted to invest in his own new initiatives and impose change quickly from the top. He considered the Bank's annual administrative budget, already above one billion US dollars, was too rigid, constrained by the Board, locked in past commitments, and inadequate for accommodating his new initiatives.

Wolfensohn was trying to get the Board's approval to a "Strategic Compact" (thereafter, Compact) whereby he would redeploy funds locked in ongoing programs, and get a one-time significant increase in the Budget. The main thrusts of the Compact were: refocusing the development agenda; revamping the Bank's information systems and processes; and redeploying resources to the field. The Compact argued for a holistic approach and long-term view that emphasized social sectors and aimed to strike a balance between growth and equity. It also called for decentralization of staff and redeploying budgetary resources away from the back-end processes to the front-end services to client countries. It envisioned a knowledge Bank, one that thrived on partnerships and country-centered ownership of development programs. These thrusts were deemed critical to the Bank's evolving role in the digital age.

I proposed the creation of a Strategic Forum, a Bank-wide gathering of senior managers to discuss strategic corporate-wide issues and to agree on broad strategic directions and resource allocation. I hoped for a participative process that would break silos and promote vertical and horizontal communication. The Forum proved very useful in bridging the gap between the President and his senior managers in owning the reforms.[15]

My twice assignments in corporate strategy convinced me that strategy implementation is much more demanding than formulation. The task of implementation was made more challenging by the complexity of the Bank's governance, organization, and scope of services. Few leaders at the Bank were experienced and adept at managing strategic change, let alone guiding deep transformation of processes and services. I was not in a position to do more than advocacy for change, and analysis on demand. I was more excited by the promise of institutional renewal than by the demands for transformative leadership. Engaging well-known strategy consulting firms may have helped with financial and institutional analysis, but fell far short in understanding the operations of the Bank and its client relationships, and in facilitating implementation by coaching the Board and top leaders to manage strategic change. Restructuring the organization into an unfamiliar matrix form was not a substitute for harnessing other interactive levers of organizational transformation.

A key lesson I took from these twice contrasting corporate strategy assignments is the fundamental role of the CEO (and his close advisors) in shaping corporate strategy. The Bank's corporate strategy was far more influenced by the CEO's vision of the future of development and the Bank's role in global development—much more than by cold analyses, complex processes, and internally-focused data. Conable's unarticulated vision was of a downsized Bank, coping with a declining business (graduating countries), and used by borrowers as a last resort for finance. At the annual meeting of IMF-WBG, celebrating their 50th anniversaries,

[15] In an exit poll, many of the participating managers expressed satisfaction and endorsed it.

international NGOs were calling for "fifty years is enough"! In contrast, Wolfensohn's Bank was one of a growing, thriving, and innovative Bank, willing to enter into new roles, products, and services. The Bank was strained and challenged, but strived for remain responsive and relevant to its clients and shareholders. Corporate strategy was a key tool to articulate and operationalize this challenging vision and its priorities. I felt at home with this second vision.

My experience with strategic planning was critical to shaping my thinking and practice of digital development. It increased my appreciation of the ubiquitous role of knowledge and communication in organizations and development processes. Ownership of policy reforms relies on information and communication between all stakeholders. In large professional services organizations like the Bank, data, information, and knowledge resources are vital to their management, effectiveness, and service delivery. Inclusive development requires empowering the weak and disadvantaged partners with timely data and knowledge (Hanna and Picciotto 2002).

My successes in influencing the VP to pioneer new strategic planning processes such as the Strategic Forum raised insecurities and jealousies. I had to work directly with the VP, who preferred to work with senior staff without much bureaucratic layers, and was keen to get my direct advice on introducing the Strategic Issues Agenda and Forum. As a new VP function, it faced many demands and uncertainties and called for new skills, creativity, and interaction, rather than reliance on traditional routines and hierarchies. There were too much rivalries between the planning and budgeting directors. In the end, I received a letter of achievement from the President. I do not apologize for the reforms I introduced with enthusiasm and VP support. However, I was subsequently asked to look for another job. As one of the managers' explained, I was too innovative to be managed!

In 1998, Robert Picciotto, Director General (DG) of the independent Operations Evaluation Department (OED), invited me to join his staff and focus on evaluating the development effectiveness of the World Bank as a whole. This assignment excited me. I had read many OED reports since I joined the Bank, ranging from evaluating single projects, to evaluating whole sectors, and to reviewing decades of Bank relationship with countries. Much could be learned from evaluating Bank and country development practice, especially when evaluation is done jointly with all stakeholders in the country. The Bank was at its best in learning from evaluation when it was open to learning and supportive to experimentation.

Unfortunately, the Bank's learning culture left much to be desired. Most glaring learning gap was in the new sectors where such learning was most needed. OED was too late in evaluating the Bank's effectiveness in assisting clients with digital transformation. I proposed undertaking an independent review of this new and fast-evolving cross-sector digital transformation, but OED management was reluctant and unprepared to address such dynamic area of assistance, except perhaps in the telecommunication sector.[16]

I led the Annual Review of Development Effectiveness (ARDE) of the Bank. Picciotto was aware of my work in strategic planning. He had strong and enduring institutional loyalty and the longest uninterrupted service at the Bank. Although Picciotto shared much of the vision of the President, Wolfensohn was skeptical of independent evaluation. Wolfensohn wanted to show timely results arising from his reforms and initiatives. Picciotto had the mandate to report directly to the Board. For me, this promised to be a challenging and learning-intensive assignment. I was eager to contribute to the strategic management of the Bank, and perhaps the OED was a better place to do it.

For the ARDE exercise, I adopted the theme of measuring Bank performance against the principles of the Comprehensive Development Framework (CDF), launched by the President in January 1999. These principles called for the adoption of a long-term view of development strategy that in addition to economics, included governance, institutions, country stakeholders' ownership; partnership with aid agencies; and progress evaluation based on poverty reduction and shared prosperity. Despite some skepticism among the hard-core economists of the Bank, the President was convinced that these principles would provide a new way of thinking about development, correct past excesses of donor-driven policy conditionality, and put the country in the driver's seat in formulating and implementing its development strategy.

The stakes were high, as the evaluation function had its own methodology for evaluation which relied on criteria and results from project completion, often after 5–10 years of project funding approval. The CDF may have represented a new consensus on development assistance among

[16] One exception was the relatively recent report (World Bank 2021).

aid agencies, but how far was the Bank and other aid agencies from living up to these principles? My own experience and my reading from past OED evaluation evidence suggested that these principles are valid but not commonly practiced. The ARDE review indicated that the Bank was far from practicing what it preached and proposed some suggestions to overcome the constraints to implementing these principles. I believed every effort had to be made to ensure that the CDF would not become yet another slogan or Washington-born blueprint to be sold to Bank clients. Reforms to incentives and culture within the Bank would be necessary to translate "theory" into practice.[17]

Much of the learning to practice these principles has informed my research and practice of digital transformation. I worked with a number of leading researchers from the Bank, the Institute of Development Studies, the Overseas Development Institute, and Oxford Policy Management, among others, to examine CDF implementation issues. These issues ranged from policy learning, mainstreaming participation, the role of democratic decentralization, and programmatic aid. This research resulted in a co-authored book on *Making Development Work* (Hanna and Picciotto 2002). I was privileged to connect with a vast and thoughtful development evaluation community.

I draw a few takeaways from practicing strategic planning and corporate evaluation at the Bank:

- Strategic planning has to shift from rigid documentation to agile, interactive, issues-driven, and communication-intensive processes.
- Strategic planning and management go beyond strategy formulation, to include orchestrated changes in governance, structure, leadership, skills, incentives, and culture.
- Open leadership and management culture should be nurtured to support learning, strategic thinking, foresight, and long-term view of development.

[17] Some of the converts who tried to demonstrate allegiance to this new consensus did not like my key message: the CDF is easy to understand and accept, but hard to practice. They feared that our candid and reasoned analysis of the constraints to practicing the CDF principles would reinforce the already existing institutional resistance to new practice. Yet, I believed institutional and political economy constraints to such practices as stakeholder ownership and co-learning with clients must be systematically identified and addressed. The converts behaved as if these principles were a matter of faith, to be practiced without questioning.

- Bottom-up innovation, private sector entrepreneurship, and multi-stakeholder feedback should be integral to leadership-driven strategy formulation processes.
- The Bank needs to differentiate its services and redeploy its staffing and budgetary resources to fit strategic groupings of countries and build up promising services.
- Independent evaluation is a critical function for strategic planning and management, institutional learning and transformation—but requires open culture.
- Aid agencies are far from practicing what they preach: taking a holistic and long-term view, securing country ownership and stakeholders collaboration, practicing strategic partnerships, and evaluating and learning throughout their collaboration with clients and partners.

Understanding Demand for ICT Applications

I consider myself a development economist, or rather a development practitioner and futurist with a multidisciplinary background. I ventured into the new field of ICT from the "demand" side. I wanted to speak economic development language to ICT specialists (supply side), and technology application language to mainstream economists and other sector specialists (demand side). This desire was at the heart of my journey of cross-disciplinary inquiry, learning, and communication.

As there was no natural home for this new approach to development, I organized a Bank-wide ICT Task Force with practitioners from the main sectors of development. We drew a "manifesto" about the *Role of the Bank in the Information Age* (Hanna 1990) that was widely disseminated to senior management and staff. This "grassroots" initiative was complemented by publishing two reports: *Information Technology Revolution and Economic Development* (Hanna 1991) and *Information Technology in World Bank Lending* (Hanna and Boyson 1993). The reports revealed that the dollar value of ICT components of Bank-funded projects has been rising, and when combined with stand-alone ICT projects amounted to a significant 10% of all Bank investment lending.[18] These components

[18] These are composed of 2% investment in stand-alone ICT projects and about 8% in total component investments.

were present in 70 to 90% of investment projects. ICT was claiming a large share of development financing and has become a significant factor in project performance.

To strengthen my advocacy of mainstreaming ICT in development, I studied industrial countries' policies and programs for the *Diffusion of Information Technology* (Hanna et al. 1995) and the relationship between the *East Asian Miracle and Information Technology* (Hanna et al. 1996). I initiated a dialogue with senior officials in several developing countries to help them build on their initial success in the ICT sector, and to adopt a strategic approach to ICT mainstreaming across the economy.

Rethinking Development: A Staff Manifesto

There was a growing unease among Bank Operations staff (client-facing services) about the Bank's response to the digital revolution. I interacted with the end-user technology teams who pioneered assistance to Task Team Leaders (TTLs) and to ICT and public sector organizations of borrower countries. I thought it was time for the technical staff to raise this issue with senior management. My own ITF management was supportive of helping public sector organizations in client countries, as long as ongoing support was invisible to senior management.

I organized a voluntary task force from all managerial complexes of the Bank. Collectively, its 40 members had extensive knowledge of information technology and borrower's needs. We met informally over "brownbag" lunches I chaired and prepared a report that focused on ways ICT improves resource allocation, productivity, institutional management, and the economy at large. We hoped that our report (Hanna 1990) would become the foundation of the Bank's response to the emerging challenges of leveraging ICT for development[19] and stimulate a Bank discussion of ways to assist borrowers in using ICT for development.

The Bank was not expected to become "everything to everyone" but to devise an approach based on its comparative advantage. The task force

[19] I prepared the report in 1990. It was distributed internally as a confidential draft. I prepared the report in 1990. It was distributed internally as a confidential draft. Hanna, 1990. *Development in the Information Age: An Evolving Role for the World Bank.* World Bank, Mimeo. A sanitized complement was published by the Bank as working paper. Hanna, 1991. *The Information Technology Revolution and Economic Development.* World Bank Discussion Paper 120. Washington, DC: World Bank.

also identified elements of a Bank-wide strategy and suggested several steps the Bank could take to meet the growing demand for assistance in the relatively underdeveloped area of ICT applications. The paper was a staff manifesto calling for Bank action at a strategic level reflecting the enormous potential of the ICT revolution and the need to address the challenges it posed for borrowers. Until the 1990s the Bank was reactive, and some argued, had missed the boat.

The manifesto made the case for Bank action. The Bank's engagement in all economic sectors allowed it to deal with cross-cutting dimensions of development. It had a global mandate to share best practice, enjoyed access to high-level policy makers, and could offer lending at scale and technical assistance. The manifesto suggested ways to mainstream existing ICT applications in Bank operations and link the many global practices within the Bank, such as industry, education, telecom, and public sector management. It also proposed to fill existing gaps in assistance by supporting economy-wide ICT strategies, sector-specific ICT applications, as well as ICT sector policies and institutions. The task force also proposed centralized policy coordination, ICT training for development practitioners, and partnerships with external stakeholders and aid agencies.

I authored a companion paper on the growing impact of ICT on the world economy (Hanna 1991). It drew on the experience of developing countries in applying ICT to all sectors of the economy and used case studies to demonstrate the growing role of ICT in development. Information explosion in advanced economies contrasted with the information poverty of developing countries. This information poverty was evident everywhere: from government policy design and decision-making to small business market dynamics, isolating communities and entire countries from global knowledge.

The paper suggested ways to leverage ICT to make the most of the scarce managerial and institutional resources of developing countries by creating new capabilities for learning and adaptation. Technology could be used as a powerful tool to simultaneously integrate and decentralize. Governments would become information providers and users, facilitate technology diffusion in SMEs, enable technical education, invest in and regulate ICT infrastructures, and catalyze policies for the ICT industry.

30 years later this paper—a task force team effort—is still cited regularly. After a major Bank reorganization, I moved from the corporate strategy function to a staff function to set information technology

policy for internal management of the Bank. Once I realized the magnitude of Bank lending to ICT components in various projects and got educated about the potential of ICT for economic development, I became convinced of my need to return to the Bank's lending operations, to deal directly with borrower countries and assist them in using ICT to speed up their development process. I was inspired by the role of ICT in the accelerated development of several East Asian countries. But there were few choices to enter this new field of "ICT for development" in Bank operations. Then, specialists were focused on telecommunications or component ICT applications in established sectors. I could not find any positions available that would deal with ICT as a sector or as enabler of new development strategies. I accepted to take a down grade to move to Bank operations and satisfy my convictions of the central role of ICT in the future of development.

As the information age unfolded, I was keen to move beyond attempts to influence policy makers through research on a meager budget and roll up my sleeves in the field.[20]

Challenges of ICT in Development Projects

It came as a surprise to senior Bank management that ICT was increasingly present in lending operations, amounting to about 10% of the Bank's investment lending and present in 70–90% of these operations, as demonstrated in a pioneering 1993 study (Hanna and Boyson 1993). We established a database for all Bank projects that helped us analyze regional and sectoral patterns in digital applications lending assistance. It demonstrated that ICT has become a dynamic "business" area for Bank lending and technical assistance that was not fully reflected in aggregate lending levels. The study was a milestone in advocating more effective management of ICT in Bank lending and maximizing its development impact.

What about digital dividends? We used Bank task managers' evaluation reviews and structured surveys to measure both quantitative process improvements and qualitative perceptions of process owners—Bank task

[20] We had to await the Bank's World Development Report of 2016 on *Digital Dividends* to get any substantial research budget and resources to do more in-depth research in this new field.

managers. Major areas of impact were targeted: trade and tax administration; public sector institutions and infrastructure modernization; poverty alleviation; and client-centered services. The majority of task managers surveyed felt that ICT was critical to achieving project objectives. But they could not afford to provide the appropriate budget and skills to improve the ICT components of their projects and to codify best practices across all projects, beyond the privileged few.

The study identified "successful" ICT investments at the operational frontier as well as common pitfalls and constraints to effective adoption and broad diffusion of new technologies. Many of these pitfalls were not unique to Bank-funded projects, but institutional weaknesses and information gaps in developing countries emphasized the importance of improving the policy environment, best practice sharing, local skills building, as well as infrastructure and support services roll-out to realize and sustain the payoffs.

ICT applications were growing in complexity and risk (high-risk, high payoff investments). It was tempting for the Bank to "throw money at the problem" by adding ad hoc computerization components to its loans. Little time and budget were given for ICT specialists to understand the business processes and organizational context that the ICT components must serve or change. Management was reluctant to invest in new ICT staff and relied excessively on short-term external consultants to address the inevitably narrower but complex issues of procurement.

The issue was no longer whether the Bank should be engaged in ICT lending. The Bank and other aid agencies were already engaged in substantial ways that challenged the quality of their overall assistance portfolio. The Bank had to live up to the expectations and aspirations of its client countries—to leverage digital technologies for inclusive development on a livable planet.

CHAPTER 4

Responding to the Digital Revolution

Abstract Did the Bank support client countries in rolling out new technologies, building communications infrastructures, and investing in information resources for sustainable development? What factors were influential in recognizing and responding to country needs and demands for digital development assistance? The author organized a Bank task force to examine ICT role in Bank lending, and drafted a staff manifesto that was presented to the Bank's senior management and disseminated widely among staff. The task force advocated a proactive approach to apply digital technologies across sectors in Bank-funded development projects. Building ICT assistance competencies would be critical to the Bank's future relevance and the quality of its portfolio across all economic sectors. Systemic constraints were identified to mainstream digital development.

Keywords ICT in Bank lending · Digital development assistance · Bank response · Digital applications

N. K. Hanna, *Economic Development in the Digital Age*,
https://doi.org/10.1007/978-3-031-54569-6_4

Toward a Knowledge Bank

In 1987, the Bank had just completed a major disruptive reorganization. As a result of this reorganization, all staff lost their jobs and had to apply for new jobs in a restructured Bank. The selection process started with the Bank's President selecting his VPs who in turn selected their immediate subordinates, and the process went on in a cascading fashion. The premium in this frantic job search was your contacts, that is, *who you knew*. This produced many mismatches as there was no time for reviewing past records or taking bank-wide interest in strategic skills and team building. It also led to a culture of mistrust, and a significant shift from institutional to personal—and at times tribal—loyalties.

At the time, I was acting chief of institutional planning (corporate strategy) of the Bank. The new senior VP for the policy and strategy complex (including a new corporate strategy department) had announced earlier he did not believe in a corporate strategy function, as it was often a sign of a declining corporation. In contrast, I had advocated to the chairman of the reorganization's task force to strengthen the strategy function, drawing on my survey of best practices in strategic planning and management (Hanna 1985). The chairman agreed but was not in control of the implementation of this "institutional renewal". Instead, the newly appointed VP decided to abolish the planning unit I was heading. He wanted to recruit one of his contacts from outside the Bank, not "contaminated" by the Bank's management culture. He did not interview any of the existing staff for the new department.

I had to quickly find a new job in the reorganized Bank. Like others in a vast pool, I had to look for a match with my contacts. My corporate strategy function was in the Financial complex, outside Operations and Administration. My former boss had left the corporate planning function earlier to the Information, Technology and Facilities (ITF) Department, and he invited me to join as Chief of Staff (an odd title introduced by the reorganization) for Information Management of the Bank. The director of ITF thought that my experience in introducing corporate strategy at the Bank would be an asset in drafting a strategy for information technology for a transformed Bank. This was the start of my journey of learning about the new information technologies and the managerial challenges they pose in large organizations like the Bank.

As the chief of staff for the Bank's information management (1987–1990), I experienced first-hand the challenges of sharing information across institutions and integrating ICT into the Bank's own management and services. The digital revolution was increasingly felt at all levels, yet the Bank was cautious and often resistant to it. Concerns about information sharing, skill gaps and role changes, bureaucratic and information power, and the inability to measure quick dividends in quality and productivity (the productivity paradox) all played a role. It took complementary investments in skills and institutional change processes for the Bank to move toward becoming a "knowledge Bank".

The reorganization opened up a one-time increase in budgetary resources and staff changes that the director for ITF saw as an opportunity to introduce desktop "computers for all", and a first email system. The corporate budgeting department was resistant to such increases in spending on information and communication facilities, citing in particular the growing concern about the lack of evidence of the productivity impact of ICT investments. Computers were still seen as word processors for secretaries while management information systems (MISs) were only for senior managers. Researchers relied on mainframe computers and in-house software applications. The Bank was not geographically decentralized enough to call for a leapfrog in telecommunications and relied heavily on fragmented systems.

The technological tsunami was creating opportunities and challenges. Much of the Bank's drafting of reports and decision documents would be done on staff laptops while traveling in the field. Information systems would communicate and data would be shared across the Bank. But resistance to change was still common, particularly among senior staff and senior managers. Different operating software standards created "standards wars" and isolated information and communications islands and fiefdoms. Information was power, particularly when it was about sharing administrative budgets and their usage to meet lending targets. A newly established "Information Resources Council" was trying to address many of these issues. As a secretary to the council, I had to document the long debates and decisions of the council. These documents were critical in negotiating solutions among senior managers and fiefdoms in a hierarchal organization. The Council was no match to the challenges in terms of authority or resources. The technology was evolving, but the challenges were managerial. Technologists often reinforced turf issues.

Should the Bank help client countries to harness their ICT and information resources for enhanced productivity and performance? End-user support teams were trying to help Bank staff to adopt the new productivity tools. Substantial organizational resources were increasingly devoted to this technological and managerial learning, and to end-user (staff) support. The Bank increasingly claimed to be a knowledge organization. Should the Bank build on this learning and devote more end-user support to countries? The Bank was already assisting and reforming the telecommunications sector. Should it now extend its assistance to ICT use in all economic sectors?

Given the challenges that the Bank was facing internally in mastering new technologies, I thought it was critical for the Bank to help client countries cope with similar challenges and support the necessary institutional changes and learning that must accompany radical technological change. Some managers argued that the Bank should not preach what it could not master or practice! Others argued that the Bank could not become a knowledge Bank without investing in knowledge partnerships and information infrastructure of its clients. The ITF management discretely created a small end-user team to help meet part of this growing client demand. Fearing possible objections from the Operations part of the Bank, ITF management did not have a formal budget or organization to deliver such services to the clients of country directors. They had to use chargeback on other services and other budgetary gimmicks to respond to a promising new area of development assistance.

A glimmer of hope came in October 1996 at the Annual Meeting of the World Bank. In front of some 170 finance ministers, Wolfensohn boldly stated that the Bank would be sharing its knowledge with the world: it was to become "the Knowledge Bank". The Bank was staffed with highly educated individuals who over the years amassed vast experience on what did—or did not—work in accomplishing its mission of poverty reduction. But this experience was mainly lodged in the minds of individual experts. It was thus difficult for other staff, let alone country clients, to benefit from this knowledge, unless they were getting a loan from the World Bank. Wolfensohn proposed to demolish these constraints and make the Bank's knowledge systematically available to anyone who needed it, both inside the World Bank and outside.

With the fast-expanding coverage of the Internet, the idea of knowledge sharing within organizations was just emerging as a hot management topic. To capture this potential, Wolfensohn pushed for investing in the necessary systems, in Washington and worldwide, to enhance the Bank's ability to gather development information and experience, and share it with clients. In March 1997, this bold vision was formally adopted by the Bank board of directors as part of a multi-million-dollar strategic compact. This was a major cultural change for the Bank: from marking most important documents confidential to a culture of open data and intensive investments in information and external communications.

Wolfensohn pushed for investments in the Bank's own telecommunications, systems renewal, and knowledge management. These investments demonstrated their value with the subsequent creation of the Open Learning Campus and the shift to remote work during COVID-19. Still, much of this potential remains to be realized due to complex non-technological—behavioral, cultural, learning—constraints within the Bank and in the client countries. We learned that knowledge management has limitations in capturing tacit knowledge. Perhaps less appreciated but equally critical is the fact that the Bank is just one knowledge-generating actor among many others in an ever-expanding network of development partners.

Some of these lessons are relevant to client countries, building their information infrastructures, knowledge management, and digital transformation systems. Internally, the Bank was able to deploy digital transformation and knowledge management systems, but as demonstrated throughout this book, this experience was not made available to client countries developing their own information policies, and ICT strategies, systems, and infrastructures. The Bank also fell short in assisting countries to harness digital technologies at a national scale.

Other aid agencies, bilateral and multilateral, have gone through similar organizational learning while building their in-house communications and knowledge management systems before their managements felt confident about assisting client countries in digital transformation. Often, the staff who worked on information technology in support of internal management within the aid agency (CIO office) were subsequently deployed to support ICT applications in developing countries. This often led to a very narrow technical approach to digital development that ignored the broader policies, strategies, and capabilities of the client country. It also reinforced common misconceptions about digital development assistance as a purely technological issue that can be treated in isolation of country assistance strategies. The learning challenges facing developing countries are much broader. They require a more holistic approach to development beyond the technical skills required to manage technology at a relatively developed aid agency.

How Did the Bank Respond?

The Bank's response to the need for digital assistance has been cautious and reactive. It relied excessively on short-term consultants to address ad hoc TTL requests. Core competencies developed slowly—in isolated pockets across the Bank, with little institutional support. Moreover, the Bank did not leverage its core strengths in policy and strategy (apart from telecommunications). Opportunities to provide strategic assistance were missed and support requests were rejected. The Bank was not perceived as a thought leader in this dynamic field. "Learning by doing" required building skills, incentives, career streams, and professional "ICT for development" expertise—the Bank did not invest in these prerequisites.

Senior management reaction to the Bank's mixed performance was often counter-productive. In the Eastern Europe and Central Asia (ECA) Region of the Bank, for example, several countries launched massive computerization and process reengineering to reform and modernize their banking, tax administration, social security, logistics, public expenditure management, and public services—a massive investment in ICT, change management, and policy reform. The Bank tried to respond to this demand but got quickly frustrated by the rising incidence of mis-procurement, corruption, and implementation delays. The ECA region's small ICT unit was struggling, so the ECA VP put a lid on the situation by declaring a moratorium on all ICT financing across the board. Neither the need, nor the risks went away.

Apart from telecommunications practice, a small group of ICT specialists at the Bank was designated to respond to growing demand, with little time for quality improvement or adoption of best practice. They were first located in the administrative support of the Bank, outside of the operational units, then joined operational staff but remained outside of and invisible to country assistance management. They were few specialists, less than one percent of the operational staff. They were often called in at the final stages of project design or during implementation to address relatively narrow technical issues—too late to capture innovation opportunities and sector-wide challenges. Cross-practice support (from ICT specialists to sector task managers) was underbudgeted and even discouraged. There were no career paths for ICT or "hybrid" staff who combined development (business) knowledge with ICT expertise. Social sectors like health and education where ICT investment was smaller and payoffs less visible lagged behind other capital-intensive sectors.

There are exceptional examples of methodical digitalization projects, led by the few ICT specialists who became well-versed in applying digital technology to selected core areas like tax administration, public expenditure, and financial management. These notable exceptions are the outcome of partnership between sectoral and ICT experts, and tolerance of country director to risk taking within the Bank, and the strong desire and ability of country borrower to pioneer investments in digital transformation.

Gradually, there has been growing realization of the limits of an ad hoc approach to ICT applications in the Bank's portfolio. Several innovative and well-prepared ICT applications in development projects were led by ICT specialists or hybrid staff in broad areas such as modernizing public administration and service delivery. But there was (and still is) a growing gap between best practice and common practice. Several follow-up studies by the Bank's Internal Audit Department and Quality Assurance Group, among others, pointed to these shortcomings and called for a determined effort to improve Bank-wide leadership in digital applications, upgrade current skills, and focus on the development of a corporate-wide digital assistance strategy.[1]

Despite demonstrated value and country demand for Bank engagement in digital assistance, there were no incentives or mechanisms to scale up and diffuse successes beyond the confines of specific ICT components of projects. There was little accountability for quality in design and implementation of these ICT components. Experts' attention was focused on creating islands of excellence in digital transformation that may eventually lead to economy-wide transformation. This rarely happened since these privileged applications were not integrated into the country's digital transformation ecosystem, nor the national economic development strategy.

Responding to Country Demand and Ownership

Why were aid agencies late to respond to the digital revolution and the growing country demand for digital transformation support? I take the case of the Bank since it is where I had most of my journey.

[1] See, for example, IAD, 1998, "Report on Follow Up Review of Informatics," World Bank.

Since the late 1980s many Bank managers perceived a *lack of demand for digital assistance* from client countries, with the exception of ad hoc investment in stand-alone ICT applications and telecommunications infrastructure. Bank managers were surprised to learn that by the early 1990s, ICT applications have already spread to most economic sectors supported by the Bank. Responsive project managers reacted to the specific country demands to invest in the modernization of their operations and services. But these ad hoc investments did not address the policy and infrastructure foundations of the digital economy. They did not deal with digital transformation at the strategic and economy-wide level. There was no apex institution or ministry with the mandate to aggregate these ad hoc ICT applications or address the underlying foundations for digital transformation. Even when demand came from relatively advanced clients, as in the case of India, the Bank did not see itself in a position to support digital policy reforms or public–private partnerships in this space.

Did *ideology* blind us from acknowledging client needs? At the Bank and elsewhere, aid managers felt this nascent industry should be left to the private sector to lead, for fear that governments would interfere with market forces. The industrial policies of many East Asian countries were not popular at the Bank, especially during the market fundamentalism period of the 1990s. Senior Bank economists were the most skeptical and did not see the rationale for prioritizing support for ICT. As a regional chief economist quipped: "There is no difference in developmental impact between producing microchips and potato chips"!

Did Bank managers view the demand for digital assistance as a *mission creep*, an unfunded mandate beyond Bank skills and comparative advantage? Did they view digital development as an unwelcome addition to an already overstretched development agenda? Did major shareholders fail to see the link between the ongoing digital disruption and inclusive growth and sustainability? Did this area of assistance lack constituencies within and outside the aid agencies? Would increasing the voice of Global South countries in the multilateral development banks (MDB) make them more responsive?

Did Bank managers and their country clients ignore this long-term challenge as it would require new skills and raise new personal and institutional risks? Did they feel disempowered to venture into a new field of assistance?[2]

Was there adequate ***accountability*** mechanism within the Bank and client countries for missing opportunities to address this technological revolution? Other factors may have contributed to denying or missing client demand. The digital transformation ecosystem ***cuts across sectors***, while aid agencies and governments are organized in silos by sector. Hence, there were ***no focal points within the Bank and country clients*** to discuss ecosystem development or supply/demand coordination. Only the most advanced transforming countries registered their economy-wide or cross-sectoral demand for ICT assistance through ministries of finance or economy, or the chief executive of the country. These demand signals, including specific requests from ministers that I passed on to management, were ignored. At times I was even accused of mobilizing this demand myself!

Demand for assistance in this new cross-cutting dimension of development has been partially driven by the interest of major shareholders of the Bank. Most instructive is Bank experience in responding to global climate change. I recall vividly how the Bank responded to a request of the Indonesian minister on environment to examine the impact of Bank-financed projects on the fragile environment of Java. The Bank's answer: we do not have experts or department in this field, but will send you our sole environmental advisor for a brief visit. In this case, Indonesia anticipated a challenge in the early 1980s and the Bank was a lagger.

Despite growing awareness of this global environmental challenge, it took several decades to respond to the environmental impact of development projects and mainstream the environmental factor into development assistance. Bank response could not address country-by-country demand at the departmental level. It had to take a whole-of-the Bank approach. Even when the mandate became clear, it took a long time to realign Bank organization and incentives to bridge the gap between mandate and performance. Yet, the Bank and other international aid agencies do

[2] I was grateful to several senior Bank managers who invited me to present the case for digital development assistance at their regional staff meetings. Yet, despite their seniority, these managers felt they lacked the authority or mandate to initiate or institutionalize such assistance.

not face similar pressures from the US and other major shareholders to mainstream digital transformation into their assistance.[3]

The perceived lack of demand for digital transformation support may also be the result of *supply-driven* development assistance. This leaves new and cross-cutting programs at a disadvantage when competing for skills and resources to develop new businesses and timely responses. What comes first: the chicken or egg conundrum—do we wait for demand from the country or do we invest upfront in business development to create and articulate such demand?

A critical factor in articulating client demand is the time and resources given to *listening, interacting and learning with clients*. Interactions between the Bank's expert teams and client counterparts are often focused on *internal* processing and adherence to project blueprints. The same applies to policy "dialogue" and policy lending, where most of the time and resources are devoted to collecting data, developing elegant analytics, and writing polished reports that are consistent with the Bank's current ideology. The Bank rarely includes digital policies in its macro-policy discussion and in lending operations.

Frequent staff rotations and brief visiting mission interactions with government leaders do not help build trusting relationships and local ownership, or leave much room for learning and innovating with the client. The Bank's frequent reorganizations have moved progressively more budgetary resources from frontline operations where interactions with clients occur—to the back office, where staff feed the "beast". I was fortunate to have long engagements with clients like Indonesia, India, and Sri Lanka which helped build longer-term relationships that were critical to trust and mutual learning.

Empathy is a powerful motivation for understanding client needs and detecting unmet demand. Empathizing with the client drove me to learn more about country conditions and created opportunities to help build mutual trust and address sensitive reform issues (as in Indonesia's budgetary and civil service reforms, decentralization); propose pioneering

[3] One exception was the privatization of telecommunications and the strengthening of the regulatory framework. On the opposite side, the US government may have been lukewarm to Bank assistance to develop the ICT (software) industries in potentially-competing developing countries. More positively, USAID, DEFID, and other bilateral agencies have supported innovative uses of digital technologies for agricultural development, social sectors, and targeted poverty alleviation.

projects in new fields (as in India's software services); co-create new e-leadership institutions (as in Sri Lanka's newly established IT Agency); and build partnerships for peace (like the border industrial estate between Israel and Palestine), among others. Empathy with country-specific conditions helped me see and overcome development assistance rigidities. Empathizing with disadvantaged stakeholders opened my eyes to the needs of these stakeholders and revealed the imperative to pursue digital inclusion.

The Bank's limited responsiveness to client demand may have been exacerbated by the tendency to adopt a ***rigid, standard, one-size-fits-all development strategy***, regardless of context. This attitude overlooks the opportunities for innovation and leapfrogging inherent in digital technologies. Digital transformation is too complex and contextual to be expressed in a standard template or to be constrained by market fundamentalism that denies government a role in promoting digital innovation and diffusion in partnership with business and civil society.

Development practitioners tend to offer policy advice based on blueprints of global best practices, regardless of country context. The same stands for technology consultants armed with the best or latest technical solutions, regardless of local institutional settings and human resources. In fact, appropriate digital policy reforms and "best-fit" technology solutions are always context specific and dependent on local complements.

Best practices should not be imposed as rigid standards, without adaptation to country specificities. In my experience, it is better to present a menu of strategic options and to engage stakeholders in pragmatic policy experimentation rather than adhering to a standard "global best practice".

The recent design of ***diagnostic tools*** for digital development, some described earlier, may help countries and aid agencies avoid the pitfall of seeking standard, ready-made, "me too" digital strategies. Appropriately used, diagnostic tools can provide a forum and process for co-learning and engaging stakeholders to understand the local environment and set relevant targets and realistic benchmarks for progress.

Since 2018, there has been a major increase in assessment tools for digital economy, digital government, and other diagnostic tools for digital platforms, cybersecurity and other digital transformation ecosystem components. This is a recent trend to ground digital strategies and development assistance into in-depth analysis of country's strengths and weaknesses. As in other aid-driven advisory services, the Bank faces a fundamental choice: either to further invest in its diagnostic tools to reinforce independent assessment of the countries policies and institutions, and capture data for sophisticated comparative analyses across countries, or to invest in new tools and modalities that would engage various local stakeholders in candid dialogue, and allow for joint and participatory diagnosis and assessment process with the Bank's clients.

Aid agencies tend to favor the unilateral control of assessment, to seek more objectivity, conduct due diligence, and eliminate the "human bias". This choice tends to lead to designing excessively complex assessment tools, extensive data collection, excessive reliance on external expertise, assessment "fatigue" among client countries, and delays in reforms and change management. A balance should be struck in favor of using assessment tools to strengthen client ownership of the process and results, facilitate dialogue among local stakeholders, and create an environment for shared vision and mutual learning.

Avoiding standard rigid policy and investment blueprints will likely increase the demand for analytic and advisory services—to engender ownership, situational awareness, and holistic thinking. Depending on how these diagnostic tools are used, they could either empower clients or lead to cognitive over-reliance and dependency. The outcome depends on the attitudes and skills of both aid providers and users. Current aid agency processes are subject to bureaucratization, excessive documentation, rigid standardization, and aid provider's unilateral control. Country-led diagnostic approaches should build on local learning, experiences, and innovations.

Below are some main lessons that are particularly relevant to large-scale digital transformation projects:

- Ownership can be engendered by driving change from the bottom up, through subnational pilots and judicious sponsorship from the top. Large-scale top-down institutional reforms may be difficult at the outset, particularly in large diverse countries, when headquarters are far from client services, vested interests are strong, and a fear of change is palpable.
- Pilots help to implement projects on a scale where complexity and risks would be manageable and early results demonstrable.

- Strategic management of large-scale computerization programs, including the sequencing of hardware, software, and organizational change is important. Software development should precede substantial investments in hardware.
- Procurement procedures of aid agencies should be adapted to deal with the relatively unpredictable yet critical process of customized software development.
- Social marketing and image building are important to facilitate change in client behavior and to scale up institutional reform efforts.
- Digital government programs should build upon local experience with computerization and organizational change, and on the existing technical platforms and standards. Experience gained from the modernization of major institutions and strategic processes such as public expenditure management and tax administration should guide national strategies for diffusing information and communication technologies on a broader scale.
- Large-scale computerization of public institutions and building public digital platforms can play a catalyzing role in creating demand and developing local service industry capabilities in ICT training and the management of organizational change.

From Research to Advocacy

Most of my research comes from the periphery of the Bank's organization; it was supported by my managers but not mandated by the Bank's top management or the Digital Development Department. This research was welcomed by the GICT department, as the findings could influence the visibility and demand for its staff. But GICT then suffered from a "not invented here" syndrome and was preoccupied by its ongoing business of lending for telecommunications development. Integrating ICT into various sectors was not a core competency of the department, or any other sectoral department. In-house ICT specialists were too few and too busy to even read the findings in order to use them to advocate for senior management support for this nascent but fast-growing field of development.

During the 1990s, the central economic development research department (DEC) did not have any research program in this area. The Bank's centrally funded research program was then dominated by macroeconomic policy and basic research. Researchers were more interested in getting published in academic journals than contributing to the Bank's operational work. As a new area of development, digital transformation was outside of the Bank's dominant research paradigm that relied on historical data and an established neoclassical economic framework.

Later, when I joined the Bank's Operations Evaluation Department (OED), I tried to get it to review the Bank's ICT lending portfolio to assess the Bank's readiness for digital development assistance. OED management was reluctant to do so as, outside of telecom, it lacked expertise in evaluating assistance for digital transformation. Besides, as digital applications spread across the entire lending portfolio, digital development was not perceived as a separate sector worthy of Bank attention.

My own applied research budget was too small to promote digital transformation. I was primarily accountable for developing a new portfolio of digital development projects, not research per se. Given the skepticism we faced, I tried to fill the gap in Bank digital strategies and operations awareness. I felt that operational research was a must to provide much-needed guidance to policy makers and program managers. My focus was on learning about digital transformation at the country and project level. I believed every country's digital strategy and digital lending operation was a development experiment. I also felt we should learn from experience as well as theory.

Thanks to my previous work at the corporate strategy unit, I was fortunate to have access to senior managers and to present my findings to their staff. Their reactions were sympathetic but guarded. Many felt that this area was too risky for Bank engagement. It was a matter of priorities as the Bank's corporate agenda was overloaded and many new mandates were unfunded or underfunded. Some managers expressed doubts about the Bank's comparative advantage in dealing with new technologies. Why not leave it to the private sector and the market? No one offered to lead it or to provide a home for it in their vice presidency or region. Most VPs felt it was up to top management to reach consensus and the Board to decide on priorities. They were uncomfortable and unauthorized to venture into this area.

In early 1990s, I tried to build consensus among senior managers on a future Bank role in leveraging digital applications for development. It was a "heroic" exercise, aimed to generate interest and consensus from the bottom up for such role. I worked with external think tanks like CSIS (Center for Strategic and International Studies), specialized UN agencies, the IT industries, academia, and key senior managers concerned with Bank performance in related areas such as private sector development and telecommunications. The idea was to create a Global Information Infrastructure Commission that would advise the management and staff of World Bank Group on such role and ensure it would reflect the concerns of developing countries. It was hoped that this Commission would raise awareness of stakeholders and build pressure on the Bank to become proactive and strategic in its digital development assistance. Unfortunately, by end of 1994, I had to leave my role as advocate and adviser to the Commission for an urgent job in support of the Oslo Accord in Jerusalem. Top management leadership was lacking. It took another two decades or so to mobilize trust funds and create a Bank-industry forum in support of a strategic role for aid in this fast-evolving field of development assistance.

Leadership was needed and to a certain extent it came from Wolfensohn, later.[4] Until then, there was little discussion among Bank management of the technological transformations shaping our future.The private sector VP who was also responsible for ICT for development found it most rewarding to give eloquent presentations on the subject to adoring audiences at global forums. He expressed frustration with the Bank's senior management referring to his peers as "dinosaurs" when it came to understanding this new area of development! Senior managers I appealed to—for much needed help to put the ongoing technological revolution on their strategic agenda—did not feel they had the power to change the situation.

Very few of the Bank staff were then interested in ICT role in development. Those involved in supporting the knowledge economy faced similar skepticism and challenges. At times, the skeptics viewed the emerging field of digital technologies as a competitor for budgetary resources and the limited attention of senior management.

For a decade or so, the World Bank Institute (WBI) sponsored a program on knowledge for development, which built upon OECD

[4] Wolfensohn's attention was divided over creating external ventures and spinoffs to promote ICT for development such as the Development Gateway (DG). However, he supported pioneering e-Sri Lanka, which was a first ecosystem-wide transformation project to be mainstreamed. A pity it came to his attention near the end of his tenure.

research on the knowledge economy of advanced countries, and on the Bank's 1999 World Development Report. Mainstream economists at the Bank preferred to conceive of the *knowledge economy* through the framework of research, innovation, and STEM (Science, Technology, Engineering and Mathematics) education supported by macroeconomic policies and institutions.[5] Their interest in technology was limited to the development of telecommunications infrastructure while their treatment of "knowledge" was highly conceptual, informed mostly by developed countries' experience. This approach led to many well-written reports and international conferences. With few exceptions, however, it did not affect World Bank lending operations. It raised awareness among economists of the role of knowledge and information in development, but did not fully recognize the digital revolution or provide the tools to operationalize its concepts, for example, by addressing knowledge gaps that hurt the poor.

Unfortunately, the knowledge economy movement tapered off once its leading proponent left the Bank. WBI was outside of Bank lending operations and the initiative was blamed for absorbing significant promotional, educational, and trust funds. Much of the attention went to devising knowledge and innovation indices and country rankings that used indicators borrowed from industrialized countries. This produced few well-written reports, but did not provide adequate support to bank financing and technical assistance practices struggling with the ongoing digital revolution.[6]

There were some exceptions to engage the Bank in science and technology lending operations. One example is an industrial technology development project for India that helped institutions become more responsive to client enterprises and introduced venture capital and complementary policy measures in support of innovation in industrial enterprises. Despite these results, the responsible task manger was unable to convince other country directors to prioritize such projects. Mainstream country economists remained skeptical of the role of technology policies in enhancing the competitiveness of developing countries. The task manager, one of the few practitioners covering this critical niche, opted for leaving

[5] See some relevant publications on innovation and knowledge economy at end of reference list.

[6] One exception was a series of trust-funded studies of technology institutions and factors leading to their effectiveness in promoting and diffusing industrial technologies (Goldman et al. 2013).

the Bank. Many others who were fed up with hitting their heads against the wall did the same.

I often wondered why the senior leadership of the Bank failed to understand the role of the ongoing digital revolution in economic development. Was it captive to traditional economic development dogmas like neoliberalism? Too busy with day-to-day issues and fire-fighting? Did they think technology transfer was not important to development in low- and middle-income countries or perhaps even impossible until basic needs were fully met? Maybe they were for "technology-neutral" economic development. Maybe the internal and external constituencies for harnessing digital technology were not strong enough. My own experience suggests that client demand was quite strong, starting from the mid-1980s, and growing stronger in the 1990s and beyond. Were the Bank's Executive Directors—mainly from ministries of finance—even aware of this demand or interested in helping client countries leverage digital technologies? Maybe political factors were at play here.

Admittedly, guiding a large organization like the Bank through the complexities of economic and digital development is no simple task. Successive Bank Presidents had little development background. None of them came from developing countries. Increasing layers of political appointments did not help. Apart from McNamara, who stayed at the helm for quite a long time and presided over a smaller but growing organization, Bank Presidents did not fully understand how the matrix organization worked and how project task managers reconciled standard Bank procedures and Board demands with the diverse and distant realities of developing countries.

Yet, presidential leadership mattered. James Wolfensohn started many valuable knowledge Bank initiatives, mainly through trust funds and spinoffs like DGF, but was constrained by institutional inertia and the lack of VP team consensus on mainstreaming digital technology into Bank operations. Robert Zoellick broke the internal monopoly on Bank data and provided free external access to the Bank's huge information resources, but still failed to link to Bank lending operations. Jim Kim was most fascinated by disruptive technologies and the spirit of Silicon Valley but did not graft its culture into that of the Bank.

In short, successive Bank leaders failed to translate their views of the role of technology into the Bank's core business of development and the inner workings of the institution. This would have demanded acting on the sources of institutional inertia and learning disabilities and changing performance incentives and managerial culture. It would have required an institutional learning process involving piloting, prototyping, and scaling. My experience as corporate strategist at the Bank and in advising top policy makers in developing countries made me appreciate the limits of individual leadership. Effective leaders must build partnerships and coalitions for reform. They should drive consensus and change among middle managers and administrators where communication and implementation often fail and visions die.

My conclusions for integrating ICT into development projects? Two broad sets of recommendations: institutional measures for consideration by senior management of aid agencies, and practical guidance for development practitioners and their counterparts in developing countries. Institutional measures include supporting experimentation, research, and "learning by doing"; measuring digital progress and trends; developing flexible and participatory project designs; building strategic core competencies; sharing promising practices; and deploying ICT for new development priorities such as environmental management and governance. These measures would maximize digital payoffs and sustainability by developing the skills and organizational structures to master new technologies, improving incentives for technology adoption, and addressing policy constraints to the effective use of ICT. Broadly, these recommendations anticipated those that came in the operationalization drive in the wake of the publication of the 2016 World Development Report on digital dividends. Guidance for task managers and country counterparts focus on securing early involvement in the application project cycle to ensure understanding of the contextual and complementary factors, and integrate capacity building requirements for inclusive and sustainable digital dividends.

CHAPTER 5

Examining World Bank Digital Strategies

Abstract This chapter assesses formal World Bank corporate strategies for digital transformation practice. Did these strategies address the foundations necessary for building vibrant digital transformation ecosystems? Did they cover strategic applications in key economic sectors? Were they owned by the operating regions within the Bank? Were they seriously followed, monitored, and evaluated? Did aid agencies practice what they preached?

Keywords Bank digital strategy · Evaluation · Corporate strategy · Digital transformation practice

The WBG's corporate strategy for the ICT sector has evolved over time but failed to match the fast pace of the digital revolution and to take an ecosystem view of digital transformation. I contributed to this strategy as a reviewer. The 1993 corporate ICT strategy focused mostly on telecommunications and a new private sector-led agenda. The 2002 ICT strategy made the critical decision to focus the ICT department's business strategy on the information infrastructure, and to leave out the ICT applications in various sectors to sector and country departments.

N. K. Hanna, *Economic Development in the Digital Age*,
https://doi.org/10.1007/978-3-031-54569-6_5

As information technology is a ubiquitous tool across all sectors, defining its role in sectoral projects is possible only once sectoral priorities are identified and means to achieve them agreed. The implications of this decision may have been overlooked because of the low awareness and ownership of the strategy outside the ICT department, and the lack of clear responsibility for driving ICT across the entire lending portfolio. Countries often did not know where to go for ICT assistance within the Bank.

The pervasive nature of ICT called for coordination across WBG and required cooperation at the sector and country levels. The ICT department was expected to work closely with country and sector management units to integrate information and communication policies and applications more broadly into country assistance strategies. But there were no mechanisms or incentives for such critical coordination to occur neither within the WBG nor within country management.

A follow-up evaluation of WBG performance in 2011 confirmed again that WBG contribution to the priority areas of ICT applications and skills development has been limited. These priorities have received little management attention even as they became serious obstacles to ICT diffusion and developmental payoffs. The evaluation acknowledged that the WBG's agenda of telecom reform and private investment support, while highly successful, was no longer enough to help client countries thrive in the new technological environment. It left it up to senior Bank management to make the urgent shift to ensure that the WBG's ICT skills and organizational structure enable effective strategy formulation, coordinated delivery, and effective division of labor among the WBG.

A Last ICT Sector Strategy

The last WBG ICT sector strategy was approved and published in 2012, covering 2012–2015. It stated that ICT is a fast-changing technology, hence the need to revisit the strategy in 2015 through an implementation update. Since then, however, there have been no evaluations or updates.[1]

This last formal strategy argued that the promise of ICT to reduce poverty materialized *only* during the ICT revolution of the 2000s, with the spread of mobile phones. To realize the ICT promise, countries

[1] Unfortunately, WBG management decided to discontinue the formulation of sector strategies at the corporate level.

revamped telecom regulations, opened up telecom markets, privatized telephone operators, and embarked on next-generation reforms. WBG has been most successful in fostering sector reform and attracting private investment in mobile communications. The strategy suggested to do more of the same in connectivity, with more public–private partnerships.

In the meantime, WBG lending for ICT applications has grown rapidly. The strategy acknowledged that the results have been mixed, with only about 60% of ICT applications achieving or likely to achieve their objectives. This was deemed acceptable—comparing reasonably well the average performance of public and private ICT projects. In my view, however, this high-risk/high-reward field required co-investment in technology tied to institutional reforms and change management. We had to avoid *complacency*, particularly given that the new strategy would be heavily dependent on applications supporting transformation and innovation across all sectors. But I think the ICT department was fearful that admitting high failure rates of ICT investments, particularly in e-government, would discourage the Bank from sustaining engagement with client countries in this sector.

Given the growing opportunities for ICT application to accelerate development across many sectors, the new ICT strategy was more ambitious than the last. It promised to do business differently. It would leverage partnerships with external sources of expertise and share ownership of the agenda across the institution. It would use country diagnostics to prioritize WBG intervention at the country level, to inform country interventions and promote greater selectivity. It would strengthen collaboration across WBG and become a connector of expertise for WBG clients. Perhaps most important, it promised to adopt a stronger cross-sector and cross-region *leadership* of the ICT agenda, to integrate the ICT agenda with regional and sector management teams, and to push for ICT skills upgrading across all sectors.

Development needs and opportunities demanded acting on the sources of institutional inertia, learning disabilities, performance incentives, and managerial culture. They demanded a shift toward areas where the WBG record has been weak or mixed—pointing to a need to rethink priorities, expand the digital agenda, and build greater expertise and awareness across sectors and regions. Yet, regional and sectoral digital strategy ownership remained limited.

The latest reorganizations at the Bank did not help—contributing to the lag in applying ICT to key user sectors like education, health and social protection and failing to assign sector priorities and address the key issues of ICT skills availability and staff incentives at the sectoral and global practice levels.

Toward Regional Strategies

2018–2022 saw a growing interest on the part of the Bank and other aid agencies in developing regional digital strategies—perhaps a sign of increasing interest in the digital economy within the regions. Several regional strategies have emerged, not yet operationalized into specific programs. Experiences of generating these strategies have not been shared or subjected to evaluation and implementation.

At the Bank, the Africa Moonshot initiative holds promise in view of the WBG regional management and African country leadership commitment. It is based on aggregating digital economy assessments country by country. The African Union is expected to take ownership. I had several concerns about this project. First of all, the assessment methodology did not extend beyond the digital foundations to capture opportunities to invest in strategic and innovative digital applications. Second, neither the WBG nor the African Union staff had the skills to meet the ambitious targets set by the emerging Africa ICT strategy.

Overall, as of 2022, regional strategies initiated by the WBG and regional development banks have mostly been limited to high-level presentations with little attention to implementation. This may be due to a lack of strong digital leadership institutions at the regional and country levels, political conflicts among member countries, as well as the inconsistent levels of digital transformation among countries. Yet, regional strategies offer potentially high digital payoffs for developing countries that must compete in a globalized digital economy.

The Central Asia Case

The Asian development Bank (ADB) invited me to help formulate a regional digital strategy for the Central Asia Region, in consultation with the 11 member countries. Budgetary resources did not allow building up the regional strategy on the basis of in-depth assessments of each member country, so the focus was on region-wide pillars (foundations) of the regional digital economy. I did not have adequate time to familiarize myself with each of these countries and suggested to engage Asya

Rudkovskaya, senior consultant, with the CAREC (Central Asia Regional Economic Cooperation) Secretariat to do the drafting of the strategy and facilitate country consultations. I acted as the strategy advisor to the team focusing on the overall framework and pillars, global best practices and potential digital solutions for regional sectoral clusters (ADB 2022).[2]

The CAREC Digital Strategy was intended as a catalyst for regional cooperation on digital matters and a mechanism to promote policy design, capacity building, and dialogue on the ways social and economic challenges in the region can be addressed with the help of digital technologies. During the COVID-19 crisis, digital technologies have proven essential to managing through the pandemic. A focus on addressing the existing imbalances in digital development across the CAREC region, on regional digital collaboration, and on sharing best practice can enable CAREC member countries to lay the basis for a sustainable and inclusive economic recovery. Boosting regional cooperation on digital transformation, adopting digital technologies to leverage existing ties and create new ones, and focused investment into regional interoperable digital infrastructure can help accelerate COVID-19 recovery and build back better for the future.

This regional approach holds the promise of mobilizing investment in regional infrastructure to close connectivity gaps. It can also help harmonize digital and data laws, develop and share digital skills, attract talent to the region, and strengthen the innovation ecosystem. It can help reduce regional trade barriers, promote e-commerce, improve regional digital foundations, and create interoperable digital platforms to enable transformation in the regions' sectors. These objectives have been formulated based on inputs from stakeholders. ADB (CAREC Secretariat), a regional institution, provided an effective platform for such consultations with the concerned countries.

To achieve its objectives, the CAREC Digital Strategy is expected to strengthen five interconnected pillars or foundations of digital transformation. The first pillar is leadership and governance. A coordination mechanism to ensure multi-stakeholder participation is proposed, with CAREC Secretariat as the facilitator and organizer of the process.

[2] Asian Development Bank. 2022. *CAREC Digital Strategy 2030: Accelerating Digital Transformation for Regional Competitiveness and Inclusive Growth.* Manila: ADB. http://doi.org/10.22617/SPR220042-2.

The second pillar is digital policy enablers and safeguards. These address the elimination of legal barriers to cross-border trade and harmonization of policies and standards, especially by implementing e-commerce and e-payments and establishing digital platforms within and across regional sectors. It would also involve aligning data policies across the region to safeguard data privacy, ensure transparency, and strengthen security.

The third pillar is digital infrastructure, resilience, and platforms. The regional infrastructure would be connected based on common principles of interoperability and security. Joint action would be sought to build capacity for regional resilience and a regional platform economy.

The fourth pillar is digital skills and competencies. CAREC member countries must tackle the critical issues of unemployment, migration, and brain drain from the region by developing digital literacy and advanced digital skills.

The fifth pillar is innovation, entrepreneurship, and ICT sector competitiveness. This is key to digital transformation across all sectors. Nurturing innovation ecosystems across the region would promote adoption of ICT by SMEs and others.

Finally, the strategy generated a comprehensive list of sector-wise solutions that would build on these foundations. These include fintech and e-finance solutions; e-commerce, e-logistics, and e-customs; e-agriculture and smart water management, among others. They should be prioritized at the next stage of strategy development and implementation.

The challenge remains in building regional leadership institutions and cooperation mechanisms owned by regional stakeholders. As of September 2022, a CAREC digital strategy steering committee has just been established—led and constituted by member governments and facilitated by the CAREC Secretariat. It will rely on an inclusive multi-stakeholder consultation model.

A Corporate Strategy for Digital Staffing?

Digital applications in various economic sectors have been growing in complexity. Digital policies, investments, risks, and the overall transformation ecosystem have also become more complex—demanding more specialization in digital foundations (beyond telecom) and in sectoral applications. Yet, the Bank's digital staff dominated by telecom specialists in the global centralized DDD has remained short on application skills.

Various sectoral/global practices like health or agriculture have been lacking DDD support while struggling with a rapidly growing lending and technical assistance portfolio.[3] Few hybrid staff were assigned to global practices outside the DDD while corporate sector strategies (in other GPs) failed to explicitly address their digital or hybrid staffing needs. Career prospects for digital specialists and hybrid staff remained limited, as there were no growth opportunities for them and few prospects for rotation outside their technical silos into mainstream sectoral operations.

Despite this urgent need for advanced digital or hybrids skills, the Bank did not develop a corporate strategy to attract, develop, or insource such staff. Most external technology consultants while on technology's cutting edge are often unfamiliar with client countries or the task of relating digital transformation to economic development. The Bank is thus exposed to serious reputational risks, while countries must deal with implementation failure.

Digital technologies should be considered an essential part of sector strategies, perhaps not unlike the "finance and budgeting" strategies that drive every sector's program. Digital literacy for staff and managers is critical to mainstreaming digital applications in various economic sectors. The Bank already conducts programs like "Finance for non-finance professionals" that provide basic understanding of the subject to potential managers. I believe the Bank needs similar programs—"ICT for non-ICT professionals" for sector staff and potential managers. This would help eliminate the fear of the "unknown" and capture the emerging opportunities for digital transformation at the sectoral level.

The importance and shortage of local advanced ICT skills have been recognized in digital economy assessments performed in many client countries. Countries are increasingly aware of the urgent need to build local digital capabilities, particularly to govern digital polices and digital transformation ecosystems. The public sector is at a disadvantage in attracting and retaining digitally skilled staff due to uncompetitive salaries and a lack of career development opportunities. Digital leadership and ICT staff development was a key issue in both Sri Lanka and India, who

[3] While ICT components in investment projects were estimated to be in the range of 70–90%, those developed and supervised by specialized ICT staff were likely to be less than 10%.

introduced CIO training programs. But the Bank has yet to assist countries in training their own public CIOs and other ICT government staff as part of their national digital strategies.

CHAPTER 6

Advocacy for Digital Transformation

Abstract This chapter touches upon several advocacy initiatives the author engaged in since leaving the Bank in 2005. The author continued to advise Bank colleagues and managers on the future of digital development assistance. He also contributed to the formation of advocacy forums beyond the Bank. These included building digital leadership capacity through creating an e-leadership academy; joining the Wits University of South Africa as visiting professor; contributing to various fora and think tanks such as People—Centered Internet; publishing books and articles; and serving on editorial boards. The aim has been to advocate for reforming development assistance to address the imperatives of the digital age.

Keywords Development advocacy · Digital leadership · Digital capabilities · Wits University · People-centered Internet

Starting around the year 2000, I began to think seriously of transitioning from the Bank to other affiliations. I became fascinated by the culture of Silicon Valley—with shared values like celebrating innovation, autonomy, learning, and openness to change. After visiting tech entrepreneurs, social entrepreneurs, venture capitalists, and Stanford University, I came back to the World Bank with energy and enthusiasm hoping to change

N. K. Hanna, *Economic Development in the Digital Age*, https://doi.org/10.1007/978-3-031-54569-6_6

the dominant culture of the Bank and bring attention to the digital revolution!

I began to explore “secondment” or staff exchange possibilities among the Bank, Silicon Valley networks/ Stanford University, and perhaps the University of Maryland. The idea was not to have one secondment or on–off event. Rather, it was to lay down the foundation for a broad staff exchange program in the digital sector where intellectual capital and networking are critical. It would be a knowledge-based partnership to foster close and long-lasting global community of practice.

I outlined the aims and scope of a proposal for such a staff exchange program to satisfy the interests of various stakeholders and build on the strengths of each: tech corporations, academia, and aid agencies. The overarching aim is to create an ecosystem or network to improve understanding of the roles and means to harness digital technology for inclusive development.

For the Bank and other aid agencies, the program would deepen understanding of Bank staff and management of digital transformation requirements in support of inclusive development. It would expose Bank management to the strengths of managerial and entrepreneurial culture of Silicon Valley and what it would take to build a variation of such culture. It would identify opportunities for sourcing expertise and knowledge partnerships and for building in-house expertise in this new field of development. The Bank would be expected to prioritize digital inclusion and development dividends. It would draw on the vast and currently underutilized knowledge of the Bank concerning the public policies and institutions that could shape the development and use of digital technologies in developing countries. It would improve digital development assistance in general and the digital sector in particular. IFC, the private sector arm of the World Bank Group, would be expected to play a catalytic roe in mobilizing finance for building the digital infrastructure.

For tech corporations, this partnership would help promote market-friendly environment for private investment in information infrastructure and applications. It would increase global tech understanding of emerging markets and the opportunities to partner with local digital enterprises. It may improve procurement practices for ICT in development projects. It would improve the visibility to Silicon Valley of the potential of emerging markets, and the transformational needs of developing economies.

For the academic constituency, this partnership would influence and hopefully resolve global issues concerning the emerging global information infrastructure and the knowledge-based global economy. It would help develop faculty staff and students/researchers in this new field of scholarship. It would help build case studies, knowledge bases, and research networks that are more relevant and linked to improving practice in developing economies.

The triangle of IT industry-aid-academic partners involves mutual interests and complementarities, but remains underfunded. At the time of 2000, my secondment proposal did not mobilize adequate funding from industry or other partners to proceed on a sustainable basis. But it planted the seeds for several initiatives that I and others pursued, after I graduated from the Bank, such as initiating an e-leadership academy and CIO networks, and co-founding the People-Centered Internet. Some are mentioned below.

I "graduated" from the Bank in 2005, in search of a new incarnation—with more autonomy and fewer bureaucratic hurdles to overcome. The sense of freedom was exhilarating but I still had several immediate tasks to address both inside and outside the Bank. Working with colleagues at the University of Maryland, I aimed to create a new e-leadership academy for governments in developing countries. I invited national CIOs and e-leaders to a first of its kind global conference to exchange experience and build a nascent community of practice. I was also preparing for my contributions at the forthcoming World Summit for Information Society, to be held in Tunis. And I was asked by the President of Sri Lanka to visit the country to help resolve some implementation problems that arose in part from changes in the Bank's task team leadership in charge of the e-Sri Lanka program.

My graduation afforded me more time to reflect and publish. I wrote several professional books that were waiting for their turn while I was working on the assembly line of delivering projects at the Bank. I have been traveling a lot on bank missions, but these missions were carried out against pressing deadlines. Now I was free to travel where I wanted to enjoy history, culture, and art. After decades with no time to draw and paint, I could now revel in my communion with nature and draw my favorite subject—trees—in all their forms and colors.

Since leaving the Bank, I ventured into many initiatives and engagements in support of the emerging practice of digital transformation. Often, these were short engagements, driven by passion, curiosity, and an eagerness to learn. An enduring aim of my post-Bank advisory and educational work remained: to advocate for a new field of development practice and to help empower CIOs and e-leadership institutions through open forums and learning exchanges.

Advocacy for Digital Development

I advocated digital transformation mostly through publishing books and articles, serving on various editorial boards and engaging in knowledge economy research networks. The reference list at the end of this book covers the main books and articles I published.[1] Some of my books were used as core textbook at several universities. Nevertheless, writing is a solitary undertaking, and much of the time is spent on reflection and research.

WBG managers and staff have been another target of my post-retirement advocacy. Three memorable events come to mind.

After a long career at the World Bank, including as acting chief of corporate strategy, I asked for a meeting with the **Bank's CEO**, Kristalina Georgieva.[2] Kristalina's agreement to meet with me was unusual, since in a hierarchical organization like the Bank, it is rare to have a one-on-one meeting with someone several grades higher than yourself. We met in her office in June 2018. She was warm and attentive. She took detailed notes and raised issues of her own. We shared concerns about development organizations' capacities to respond to the challenges and opportunities of the digital revolution. She followed up with an email: "Thank you very much for taking the time to visit and share your thoughts. I will follow up". She asked for recommendations of candidates to lead the new Digital Development Department (DDD) and appreciated my suggestions.

She also indicated her commitment to address the challenges we discussed. She confirmed my long-held belief that effective assistance in deploying digital technologies is essential to maintaining the Bank's development effectiveness. In a quick follow up, she elevated the ICT practice to a global DDD. The new department was mandated to help build the

[1] Some were co-authored books. Please see list of references.

[2] She was then (2019) the CEO of the Bank; currently (2024) the managing director of IMF.

foundations of the digital economy and help mainstream digital transformation across all global practices. This was a leap in the Bank's approach to digital development, but it did not address the key issue of cooperation among all sectors and global practices in support of the digital economy, and left the question of coordinated leadership at the highest levels of management unanswered. Thus, despite a step forward, the challenges of harnessing digital transformation for development remained enormous for both the Bank and its client countries.

Another memorable advocacy initiative was when Dr. Mahmoud Mohiedin,[3] *WBG Corporate Secretary* at the time, invited me to present the challenges of the digital revolution and its implications for development practice. I worked closely with young staff to enhance my slides for visual impact. Mahmoud chaired a panel of Bank directors to discuss my presentation that called for a proactive approach on the part of the Bank's senior management in line with the twin goals of inclusive growth and poverty elimination. The event held in the largest conference room of the Bank was well publicized and well attended. At the time, in 2013, DDD staff morale was low, and the senior manager, a former US government CIO, was struggling to fit in with the Bank's culture and apply his skills to address economic development priorities. This senior manager was a member of the panel. He was joined by the Africa region's director for strategy and operations and the director of the development data (statistics) department.

This was a significant event for me—a public demonstration of the divergence between what the senior managers saw as adequate WBG response and the opinions of Bank staff in attendance. The operations' director felt there was no need for specialized ICT skills for the operational team running projects rich in ICT applications. DDD's senior manager was put on the spot with a question from the floor about who was ultimately responsible for this critical area of development. Another attendee questioned why the Bank had over 700 staff managing internal information systems while the total operational staff for digital development assistance did not exceed 70 people. It was clear that the ICT skills gap across Bank staff was enormous, and the Bank's response to the digital revolution was reactive at best. With this event, I put my head in the lion's mouth!

[3] In 2016, he was the WBG Corporate Secretary and the President's Special Envoy to the UN, and since then the executive director of the IMF Board.

I also had the opportunity to work with Manu Bhardwaj, the late **US State Department** senior advisor and a passionate advocate of digital inclusion, to bring pressure from outside aid agencies to reforming their digital development practices. My advocacy was in alliance with US State Department, USAID, and a large network of Silicon Valley entrepreneurs and NGOs (PCI). Working with this coalition, we were able to get Kim, WBG President at the time, and John Kerry, US Secretary of State, to co-host a meeting of all participating finance ministers at the 2016 IMF-WBG annual meetings. The meeting was intended to raise awareness and pledge commitment to work together to ensure more inclusive and holistic access to the Internet. The high visibility of this meeting was short-lived. Kim's office did not follow up. Changes in the US administration and the State Department did not help. Busy with day-to-day management, the DDD director failed to capture this rare opportunity to gain top leadership attention and commitment to act.

One final example of advocacy was my work with Peter Knight and several Brazilian policy makers and academics as co-coordinator of *e-Brazil*. E-Brazil was initiated as an advocacy effort to build the intellectual capital and e-leadership needed to raise awareness and create a sense of urgency for a more focused e-development strategy at the national, state, and municipal levels. I did not need much convincing to participate since Brazil with its 200 million-strong population and US 1.5 trillion GDP (2020) was a major developing country with much potential facing major development challenges, such as extreme levels of income inequality and high environmental risks.[4] We wanted to advocate for strong leadership and a broadly shared vision to drive the coordination of e-development policies and programs, leverage local innovation and learning, and scale successes across the country (Hanna and Knight 2011).

The e-Brazil team reviewed international and Brazilian experience and produced public policy recommendations to achieve the country's twin goals of building a more equitable society and a more competitive economy. Team members had diverse international and political affiliations. Early on, they published a few books and held several national or

[4] I was also attracted by the natural beauty of Brazil, the creativity of its people, and recollections of my earlier visit to the Amazon (under the Bank's poverty immersion program).

regional consultations and communications conferences.[5] A presidential decree established an information technology secretariat at the Ministry of Planning. The private sector and NGOs played complementary roles in shaping the digital strategy. As *digital inclusion* became an increasingly important theme during the two governments of President Lula (2003–2011), programs in this area were developed separately by several ministries.

The Brazil team tried to engage the Bank in the early stages of this exciting journey. We were volunteers, driven by our enthusiasm to work with talented local stakeholders, and the opportunity to engage the Bank in a pioneering country partnership on digital transformation. We arguing that timely Bank assistance would strengthen government commitment to this nascent sector and specifically help address the challenge of digital inclusion. We argued the case for Bank engagement to facilitate policy reforms (in telecommunications, innovation, and digital government, among others) in a technically advanced yet politically constrained environment.

At the time, Bank management was reluctant to engage in a new sector where in-house technical skills were limited, and where an ongoing Bank lending program focused on fast and easy financial resources transfer. Bank management still viewed digital development as a private sector domain with little for the government to contribute. I felt that a weak or non-existent partnership with the government and civil society stakeholders on the national digital transformation agenda would accelerate the already growing digital and poverty divides. This was yet another missed opportunity for the Bank to learn with an advanced client and to demonstrate best practices across Brazil and Latin America.

Despite Bank reluctance, e-Brazil may have planted local seeds for a refined digital strategy developed in 2017. It took a comprehensive, integrated view of digital transformation, with equal attention to access, policy, innovation, and skills as enablers, and focused on key applications for the economy and the public sector. Through an interministerial working group, several key ministries were involved in shaping

[5] Peter and I, together with 40 others co-authored a major book on e-Brazil, published in 2006. Back in September 2000, Tadao Takahashi published a book at the Ministry of Science and Technology, known as the Livro Verde (Green Book). We aimed to build on such pioneering work and broaden ownership of an inclusive national digital strategy during the Lula administration.

and implementing digital transformation programs. The issue of strategy coordination and leadership remains an ongoing challenge while thought leadership and a national consensus on digital transformation require further work. A shared vision of a desired digitally-enabled future must focus more on the ways to leverage digital technologies to achieve Brazil's development goals. A strategic communications program grounded in the effective use of mass and social media would greatly facilitate ownership and the implementation of the emerging strategy.

Building Digital Leadership Capacity

Building digital leadership capacity has been an ongoing theme of my professional journey. I once tried to create an e-Leadership academy at the University of Maryland (UoM)—my first engagement after leaving the Bank. Working closely with professors Boyson and Wilson, we mobilized funding from aid agencies and global tech companies to fund the participation of leading public CIOs from the Global South in the first international workshop for public sector CIOs. We alternated holding the workshops at the University of Maryland (UoM) and the World Bank Institute (WBI). At a meeting I set up between these CIOs and Bank managers in charge of ICT, they pressed Bank management to be more proactive and take the lead in building digital leadership capacity. It was fitting that this discussion took place in the Bank's Executive Directors' board room.

This workshop convinced us of the need to institutionalize this format by creating a digital leadership academy either at the UoM or at the WBI. We reviewed the US government's CIO core competencies program and existing CIO curricula at certified US universities for best practices and potential modules. In most cases, executive education programs were part of elite business schools and many of the participants were CIOs of large US enterprises. It was clear to me that more tailored CIO programs were required to address the needs of developing country CIOs with equal attention to core competencies, leadership development, and cutting-edge digital technologies. Unfortunately, neither WBI nor UoM were ready to take the risk of initiating such programs without upfront funding to develop curricula, support international travel, etc.[6]

Building on this experience, I contributed to forming a regional CIO network for Asia and promoting a UN-sponsored CIO network for Africa, among other spinoffs. I also joined the LINK Centre, University of Witwatersrand, Johannesburg, as visiting professor of digital transformation[7] in its Africa-focused research program and participated as member of the Editorial Board of the Africa Journal of Information and Communication. Core competencies and networks of CIOs were being developed, going beyond the mastery of digital technologies and including people and change management skills.

Within the academic community, I tried to make the case for practical research addressing the ongoing challenges facing developing countries. But the digital development research agenda for developing countries was preoccupied by a focus on narrow, quantitative, empirically-verifiable issues, mainly concerning telecom and Internet access. Studies of country experiences in setting policies and applying digital technologies in a holistic way were often viewed as messy as they dealt with many difficult-to-quantify variables such as the political economy, society, culture and institutions. They were thus less likely to be published in Western journals.

My concern about building digital leadership capacity went beyond developing core competencies for individual leaders or CIOs to include digital leadership institutions. I surveyed leading ICT institutions and ministries in 40 countries and synthesized my findings in a paper sponsored by the World Bank's Institute (Hanna 2007). The general-purpose nature of ICT requires institutional arrangements and coordination mechanisms that ensure the coherence of policies and investments across many relevant sectors—a whole-of-government (and whole-of-society and economy) approach. There is no single organizational model or "one-size-fits-all" solution. Thus, aid agencies should help countries discover the strengths and weaknesses of alternative models.

[6] Wilson was offered a deanship at the faculty of Annenberg School of Communications at USC, and Boyson's business school was preoccupied with the more lucrative MBA programs.

[7] Working with Luci Abrahams, director of LINK of Wits University.

There were clear trends in the evolution of e-leadership institutions, moving from ad hoc processes and task forces to institutionalized engagement of core ministries, presidents and CEOs, and coordinating mechanisms that encompass key elements of the national digital ecosystem. My findings indicated the need to evaluate institutional options, promote national consensus and demand for e-leadership institutions, build the core competencies of these institutions, promote institutional innovation to engage the private sector and civil society, and design projects and implementation units with a clear view of institutionalization. Policy reform and institutional innovation are at the heart of the development process.

In 2005, the Dubai School of Government invited me to a regional conference to share research findings of a joint program with Harvard's Kennedy School of Government. I was asked to deliver the conference's concluding remarks. I came out with some important conclusions concerning knowledge partnerships and the need for developing locally-driven research capacity to advance digital transformation across the Arab region. There were no jointly authored research papers by Harvard and local scholars, no local case studies, and thus little bridging to local realities. Despite significant local experience in implementing digital government, implementation issues were ignored or treated only conceptually. Comparative studies of digital implementation at the cross-country and cross-agency level in the Arab region were non-existent.

I concluded by calling for localization of research, evaluation, and learning at the regional level, building regional centers of excellence for evaluative research, bringing a local consulting industry perspective, relating e-government to local governance and managerial cultures, developing and teaching local cases, and learning from local successes and failures. The conference's main output was a book authored mainly by Harvard professors. I was never invited back!

In Kuwait, I was asked to help establish a monitoring and evaluation function at a new national ICT agency. The country was investing heavily in ICT hardware, software, and Internet access, but with little evidence of payoffs. My interviews with physicians and educators, among others, revealed that technology access alone did not change the behavior of users or service providers—a focus on the human dimension was needed. The existing metrics of the country's national statistical system did not capture the impact of ICT investment at the micro- and macro-levels.

In 2012, at the request of the African Development Bank (AfDB), I did a review of the potential roles of digital transformation in addressing the core developmental challenges of the North African region. The region's challenges were severe: poor governance; unresponsive and rigid institutions; corruption and anti-competitive practices; unemployment among the young, educated and women; fragile social cohesion and rising inequality; educational systems that did not keep up with the imperatives of technological change and knowledge economy; and poor management of natural resources such as water, urban, and energy. Digital transformation could play an important role in addressing these regional challenges. Unfortunately, at the time, AfDB had limited in-house capacity and insufficient leadership commitment to follow up and leverage digital technologies to address the developmental challenges of the region.

Joining Global Forums and Think Tanks

A second theme of my activities since leaving the Bank was establishing or participating in various global forums and think tanks. This included the People-Centered Internet (PCI) Network; the Center for Policy on Emerging Technologies (C-PET); and the World Summit on the Information Society (WSIS II, 2005), among others.

Soon after leaving the Bank, I participated in WSIS II—the Second World Summit on the Information Society. It was a unique global event attended by hundreds of NGOs and thousands of development practitioners, along with international organizations, businesses, and political leaders. Despite turf rivalries within UN organizations and with the Bank, WSIS was a pioneering initiative to bring inclusive information society and universal Internet access to global attention. It has evolved since to become an inclusive process, led by the ITU. Unfortunately, the WSIS put much emphasis on the process, much less on implementation and outcomes. It remains a valuable global forum for inclusive participation in shaping global policies for the digital economy. However, almost two decades since WSIS II, there has been little engagement from the World Bank and regional development banks.

I became convinced that partnerships across aid agencies and taking a multi-stakeholder approach will be critical to establish global enabling policies and regulatory frameworks of the digital world. Again, the Bank was conspicuous by its absence from such multi-stakeholder forums. But the potential for productive partnership between UN agencies and development finance agencies like the Bank are likely to be high. The UN agencies would offer global forums for inclusive participation and collaborative governance, while the Bank would remain action-oriented, country-focused, and a major source for long-term infrastructure finance.

I co-founded *PCI* (*People-Centered Internet*) together with Vint Cerf, Mei Lin Fung, and Anil Srivastava. We held an inaugural meeting at Stanford University to which I invited many of my CIO contacts from developing countries. I vividly recall my presentation with the authors of the 2016 World Development Report on digital dividends that broadened the scope of the debate beyond just Internet access and placed ICT into a broad developmental context. I saw that there was a growing interest within the Silicon Valley community to contribute to global development through inclusive and affordable access to the Internet.

I was stunned by the contrast between Silicon Valley's enthusiasm and optimism about the power of ICT and the skepticism of aid agencies (particularly the World Bank) questioning ICT impact on development. But the potential for synergy via an open forum was also evident. PCI, now re-named Digital Cooperation and Diplomacy (DCD), has since operated as a network of networks where many, including myself, could share initiatives to make technology work for inclusive development. It is currently in search of ways to put digital development on the agenda of international fora like the G20, the ITU, and other UN agencies, and to promote global digital public goods alliances.

I joined *C-PET (center for policy on emerging technologies), a policy think-tank*, as senior fellow and board member. It aimed to establish a forum for business leaders, lobbyists, university researchers, US Government policy makers, and international agencies staff to exchange views on the implications of emerging technologies for public policies, jobs, US competitiveness, privacy and security, ethics, and the environment. Nigel Cameron, C-PET President, often framed the issues to provoke discussion and invite differing views. Most critical was the tension between the short-term perspective of business leaders (and their lobbyists) and the need for foresight and long-term horizons to deal with emerging technologies and their implications for the US, its competitors, and developing countries. What should be the guiding principles for Internet governance? What are the implications of artificial intelligence for jobs and shared prosperity? Data and privacy? Rising inequality? and so on. These broad issues with major societal implications cannot be left to the technologists alone.

I tried to bring Bank staff to the C-PET forum. I was surprised by how little interaction there was between US government agencies and international institutions located in the DC area on long-term strategic issues such as the environment, inequality, and the future of work. C-PET faced funding challenges since funding for non-endowed non-partisan think tanks is scarce.

At Microsoft's 2008 *Government Leadership Asia Forum*, I chaired the knowledge economy track. The forum was well attended by ICT ministers and digital economy regulators. It focused on exchanging experiences among developing countries. To me, it demonstrated the power of global technology corporations to convene world leaders to harness the technology for global good and resilience.

During this forum, I had the opportunity to engage with Bill Gates. I shared my belief that Bank and UN partnerships with the global tech corporations need to move beyond social responsibility financing and trust funding to a deeper engagement on global digital policies, public goods, and knowledge sharing for equitable digital transformation.

Evolving Conceptions of Digital Transformation

Thinking about digital transformation has evolved over the four or five decades of advocating and practicing digital development assistance. At the end of this book I synthesize the lessons I learned about practicing development for the digital age. Here, I briefly draw key shifts in this learning journey.

First, *shift from viewing cautious colleagues as obstacles, to addressing the institutional factors that are limiting them as innovators, collaborators, and enablers.* This shift compelled me to try to understand the incentives and cultural factors inhibiting personal and institutional learning. I sought to meet with senior managers such as Kristalina Georgieva (when she was CEO of the World Bank), and to focus my advocacy on senior managers across user sectors, at global forums and beyond the Digital Development Department. I still believe that there are many institutional leaning constraints to innovation in general, and to digital innovation across sectors in particular. Senior management commitment is critical to the creation of a safe and rewarding learning environment and forums to share, celebrate, and diffuse digital innovation for development (Part 3, chapter 4).

Second, *shift from an exclusive focus on the promises and opportunities of the digital revolution to acknowledging and addressing the risks of the digital world.* I admit this realization came late in my digital development practice, given the predominance of the neoliberal ideology (the market can solve all problems) at the Bank.[8] The benefits are often delayed or not realized either. The digital divide remains wide, both in access and use, reinforcing other economic inequalities. Monopolization of digital platforms has led to massive concentration of market power and exacerbated inequalities. Where governance was weak, the outcome was greater control rather than empowerment and inclusion. I feared that acknowledging these risks without adequate Bank or client country expertise would only increase Bank resistance to engaging with client countries on digital transformation.

Digital transformation practice is currently infected by the enormous power of digital monopolies and the neoliberal tenets of the World Bank. The digital monopolies who hold enormous influence over Western governments would presumably welcome expanding their markets in the developing world. But the friendly neoliberal policies also ignore information asymmetries, digital user capabilities, surveillance issues, digital public goods, and rising inequality. To counter this undue influence and address market failures, emphasis should be increasingly put on building state capacity to govern digital transformation, promote universal digital literacy, nurture local adaptation and innovation, target digital inclusion, prioritize access to basic service, and secure multi-stakeholder processes and independent evaluation, among others. The aim is to counter or minimize the distorting influences of global and local monopolies, and other risks and harms associated with the inevitable and desirable drive for digital transformation. The Bank and other aid agencies should be engaged to help countries build bargaining power vis a vis global and local monopolies and build more fair, transparent, and learning partnerships.

As the data revolution spans the globe, disruptive technologies such as Big Data, artificial intelligence, spyware, augmented reality, and virtual reality have raised the risks of cybersecurity, digital fragility, digital terrorism, state and business surveillance, and disinformation. These

[8] Neoliberalism is generally defined as free-market capitalism. It is associated with policies of economic liberalism, including privatization, deregulation, globalization, free-trade, and reduction of government role, and increase of private sector role in the economy and society.

challenges are compounded by the absence of a global consensus on addressing the issues of data privacy, censorship, and Internet governance. Building capabilities to manage these growing risks must now become integral to development assistance at the national and global levels.

Third, *shift from implementing isolated ICT components in development projects to leveraging digital technologies to transform entire sectors and economies*. This requires addressing complementary policy and institutional factors to enhance the sustainability of digital transformation projects. In the late 1980s to the early 1990s, I focused on procurement policies in ICT pilots and in large-scale computerization programs—where global suppliers held most of the "how to", user institutions did not have a clear idea of user requirements, and development dialogue was limited to interactions between technology specialists at the Bank, their in-country counterparts, and global tech companies. As technology evolved, digital payoffs were demonstrated, and aspirations rose, my attention shifted to holistic transformation, digital platforms, and portfolios of applications at the sector and country levels. A holistic, ecosystem view became necessary—with an increasing emphasis on the enabling foundations of policies, skills, and shared platforms to support a prioritized portfolio of applications.

Fourth, *a shift from short-term interventions for demonstrating payoffs and promoting quick wins to the longer term, phasing and sequencing, with sustained commitment to transformation*. While there were often opportunities for leapfrogging in technology, I increasingly realized that meaningful transformation is a long-term process, often extended beyond the time horizon of a typical aid-funded project. Digital transformation is a marathon, not a sprint. It is a process, not a destination. Exaggerated expectations and hype cycles were good for marketing, but often disappointing for new and poorly-prepared adopters. Technological and institutional learning takes time and leadership commitment to be sustainable.

Fifth, *a shift from taking for granted that ICT is crucial for sustainable and equitable development in countries at different stages of the development process, to making a clear articulation of the reasons why ICT is needed in a specific context and stage of development*. Having policy makers and development practitioners think through why their country needs digital transformation and in what priority sectors, is important not only for prioritization, but also for country ownership and partnerships. This calls for engaging policy makers (and regulators and development economists) with technology suppliers and business leaders in formulating country digital strategies in the context of a national development strategy and Sustainable Development Goals.

To those of us who have spent decades evangelizing the benefits of digital transformation and demonstrating ICT as a general-purpose technology, its usefulness seems so self-evident so as not to warrant justification, particularly since the digital revolution has been ongoing for decades—with many examples of transformed economies and applications to share. While I observed first-hand the enormous impact of ICT on people's lives in different contexts and stages of the development process, I could only illustrate it here with a few country examples. My comparative studies suggest there are many entry points and paths to digital transformation of countries at different levels of economic and institutional development (Hanna and Knight 2011a, b) and a multitude of ways digital technologies promote inclusion, efficiency, and innovation (World Bank 2016).[9]

I know from experience that the creation of an ICT-enabled country development strategy as an entry point for Bank assistance tends to meet resistance and skepticism—as illustrated in my country case studies. Digital transformation must become a core topic for policy dialogue and investment programming with concerned core ministries of finance and economy. At the same time, an ICT-enabled country development strategy is a good guide for prioritizing economy-wide digital development investments and offering a welcome source of hope and inspiration for developing countries.

Sixth, *shift from considering ICT as independent of contextual and stakeholder considerations to differentiating digital transformation strategies to fit different contexts and stakeholder priorities.* The more I applied digital technologies in diverse contexts, the more I realized the importance of a shared understanding of the context where it is applied and of the local stakeholders who will be affected. I illustrate this with the role of governance in promoting and using digital government, and the role of local leadership and multi-stakeholder participation in envisioning and implementing smart city programs. To build the contextual intelligence and ownership needed for city transformation, I had to broaden

[9] The Bank's World Development Report on Digital Dividends gives ample examples. So do several of my books listed at the end of this book, as do the testimonies of visionary leaders in pioneering countries at different levels of development.

stakeholder consultations beyond the city government to include civil society and community organizations, local universities, local industries and service companies, and at times, global tech companies and federal and foreign development partners. I learned that digital transformation is not primarily a technocratic process; it is a highly interactive, social learning process.

Seventh, *shift from an exclusive reliance on either bottom-up digital innovation or on a top-down digital strategy to a combination of emergent and deliberate strategies.* Initially, I had hoped that bottom-up innovations in applying digital technology via components and pilots would be sufficient to gain senior Bank management commitment to mainstreaming these digital applications across sectors and practices. But the level of management commitment and the pace and scale of application mainstreaming proved inadequate and I became convinced that only combining a top-down strategy for digital innovation with bottom-up initiatives will help to master digital transformation at the Bank and in developing countries.[10]

[10] McNamara used top-down strategy to mainstream urban and rural development programs and used the strategic controls of programming and budgeting and the appointment of senior change agents to implement his vision. JDW tried to do the same with the Strategic Compact and knowledge Bank initiatives.

[illegible]

[illegible]

[illegible]

CHAPTER 7

Digital Strategy for Aid Agencies

Abstract This concluding chapter explores the key factors that have delayed the Bank's and other aid agencies' response to today's fast-changing technological environment. It outlines four key elements of a strategy to accelerate learning at aid agencies: strengthening corporate leadership and strategy for digital transformation; mobilizing staff and other resources for the digital future; nurturing a learning and innovation culture; and promoting cross-sector collaboration within and among international aid agencies and country stakeholders.

Keywords Leadership · Digital strategy · Learning organization · Learning culture · Cross-sector collaboration · Progress and challenges

The imperatives of the ICT revolution and the lessons arising from case studies of digital transformation present special challenges to development assistance. Digital transformation is a process that requires sustained stakeholders' commitment to profound changes over the long term. This process involves building an enabling policy environment, leadership and institutions to govern the transformation process, and new skills and attitudes to manage technological change and innovation. It calls for coordination within governments and aid agencies to build the information infrastructures and skills for economy-wide transformation. It

N. K. Hanna, *Economic Development in the Digital Age*,
https://doi.org/10.1007/978-3-031-54569-6_7

requires a holistic view of the ICT ecosystem, covering all components of digital transformation. It also demands continual and institutionalized learning to take account of the local context and adapt to fast-changing technologies.

How prepared is the Bank to leverage the opportunities and mitigate the risks of transformative technologies? How can aid agencies address the evolving demand for new services to cope with multiple global challenges in the digital age? Why has the Bank been slow to respond to today's fast-changing technological and learning environment? How can Bank in particular learn faster to stay relevant? To me the answer is clear: they must transform into learning organizations, with innovation, effective leadership, strategic staffing, and incentives for innovation, collaboration, and results.

Drawing upon my long experience at the Bank—and my evaluation of the aid scene in general—I identified several key institutional factors that can promote or hinder innovation and learning, particularly as they apply to digital transformation[1]:

- Agency governance, leadership, and strategy;
- Staffing and strategic resource allocation;
- Culture for learning, innovation, and evaluation;
- Partnership across sectors and aid agencies.

Agency Governance, Leadership, and Strategy

The Executive Directors of the Bank (the Board), representing over 180 member countries, is expected to guide management and staff to anticipate and prepare for the future. Until about 2015, the Board did not give much attention to the opportunities and threats of the digital evolution. Technological change and its impact on economic development has been considered to be a long-term issue and perhaps not amenable to adaptation for developing countries. Understandably, the Board has been preoccupied with a huge agenda of near-term challenges. At the Bank,

[1] These conclusions are based on the specific country examples mentioned in earlier chapters, my own long experience at the Bank, the experience of colleagues who dared to break bureaucratic boundaries, and the growing literature examining aid effectiveness, including recent surveys and findings of the Bank's Independent Evaluation Group (IEG).

thinking about the future has been focused on 3- or 5-year plans. The primary occasion for considering the future role of the Bank has been when mobilizing IDA replenishments and general capital increases every few years. This is the primary vehicle for donor countries to push their agendas.

Governance mechanisms can be further strengthened to improve awareness of the long-term implications of the digital revolution, develop foresight capabilities, provide incentives and leadership signaling, and other measures to secure Bank preparedness. Recent encouraging developments include independent evaluations and policy papers produced for the Board and Development Committee on how the Bank Group is prepared to leverage the opportunities and mitigate the risks of disruptive and transformative technologies. Geopolitical tensions between major shareholders make consensus on digital strategies and global digital public goods difficult to achieve, yet the stakes are too high for all involved to ignore.

Weak corporate digital strategy and leadership at large aid agencies remains the leading barrier to responding to the digital revolution. For example, the WBG has not updated its ICT corporate strategy since 2012. There may be unit or sectoral strategies for digital transformation, but no current corporate strategy for such a dynamic, fast-growing, cross-cutting development opportunity. Earlier successive strategies, though approved by the Bank's Executive Board, were drafted by the global ICT unit. They focused mainly on telecommunications infrastructure. They left out key issues of leadership, staffing, and structure for the whole digital transformation ecosystem. They resembled a business plan for the global ICT unit only. These narrowly conceived strategies were not embraced by the operational units of the Bank, where ICT applications are often financed. Meantime, sectoral strategies for health and education, among others, left out of their scope the potential roles and challenges of the digital revolution in their respective sectors.

My 1993 study of ICT applications in the overall development portfolio of the Bank suggested that it was both feasible and desirable for the Bank to take a proactive role in supporting ICT-driven development in the information age. I even argued that developing the Bank's digital assistance competencies would be critical to its future relevance and the quality of its portfolio across all economic sectors. I was not alone in this journey. Other fellow travelers shared similar frustrations. But I felt great when I was part of a small team empowered by an influential manager.

Bank-wide leadership to support innovation and pioneer a new field of assistance was sorely lacking. The CEO of the Bank agreed—but only 30 years later!

Leadership is key within aid agencies and within each country. Leadership matters in creating an innovation and learning environment. Changes at top management to facilitate innovation also matter. Wolfensohn made a difference in promoting the knowledge Bank and in giving me the go-ahead to proceed with e-Sri Lanka. His influence, however, was indirect and came too late in my career to allow my team to replicate these kinds of projects. Jim Kim was aware of disruptive technologies and initiated a Bank response prior to his departure.[2] The selection of Digital Dividends as the focus of the 2016 World Development Report made a significant impact on many country economists who were otherwise slow to recognize the profound implications of the digital revolution for development.

Aid agency leadership and corporate strategy are essential to overcome the barriers outlined above. These barriers will not fall from a single shot but require sustained reform, capacity building, and cross-sectoral leadership. They demand cumulative and systematic learning within aid agencies and with client countries. Relying on bottom-up initiatives alone without an enabling corporate strategy could create chaos and waste resources. Active learning from past operations and systematic rehearsing of the future are a must.

Digital leadership and strategies must be driven by and embedded in overall socio-economic development strategies at the aid agency, country, and sector levels. The current prevailing practice has been to leave such leadership to the digital specialists without adequate engagement of economists and other sector specialists, such as health, education, and governance. This practice has often led to poor prioritization of digital applications and complementary non-technical investments. Accordingly, such strategies put most emphasis on investing in the latest technologies, following the "hype" cycles. They tend to ignore broader considerations to secure the policies, infrastructures, equitable access, and institutional capabilities necessary for maximum impact and sustainability.

At the Bank, digital leadership for assisting developing countries remains diffused. Who owns and leads the ecosystem? For e-Sri Lanka,

[2] But his tenure was undermined by too many disruptive organizational reforms and abrupt leadership changes that undercut staff and mid-management trust.

for example, Peter Harrold (country director, Sri Lanka), Praful Patel (Regional VP), and Mohamed Muhsin (Bank CIO) played critical leadership roles. But such a coalition of actors remained an exception. As of 2023, there is no chief digital officer or cadre dedicated to harnessing the digital revolution for development. In 2021, attempts were made to create a steering committee to bring coherence to the Bank's response to the digital revolution across all global practices. Similar attempts are being made to create a digital envoy at the UN and USAID, among others. As of end 2022, progress has been slow in building coherent Bank-wide leadership for digital transformation.

The role of corporate leadership in promoting innovation and learning should shift from an exclusive reliance on either bottom-up digital innovation initiatives (emergent strategies) or top-down, upfront directions (deliberate strategies), to a combination of both. Effective leadership would combine top-down direction for strategic innovation initiatives with creating the enabling environment for bottom-up innovations and their diffusion. It would combine long-term commitment to a transformative vision, with agile experimentation and learning. Under McNamara, new fields of development assistance, like integrated rural development and urban poverty relief, were driven top-down and articulated through a series of research and World Development Reports. Subsequently, they were systematically operationalized throughout the organization. The fast pace of change driven by the digital revolution suggests that exclusive reliance on a top-down strategy would limit the Bank's capacity for a timely and effective response to new challenges.

Wolfensohn supported bottom-up innovation and helped initiate an innovation marketplace within the Bank. He articulated a broad vision of a knowledge Bank but did not mainstream the innovations required to operationalize his vision. His leadership was decisive in enabling me to break through the bureaucracy and develop a model for an integrated digital transformation operation. But I was only able to do this at the end of his tenure when the CIO gave me sufficient autonomy and resources to collaborate with in-country reformers to pursue a pioneering project.

The role of top management in enabling change agents to innovate in new fields of assistance is fundamental. Initially, I had hoped that bottom-up innovation in applying digital technology via components and pilots would be sufficient to gain senior Bank management commitment to scaling and mainstreaming these digital applications across sectors and practices. But the level of management commitment and the pace and scale of mainstreaming digital applications proved inadequate for rapid response and agile learning. I became convinced that only combining a top-down strategy for digital innovation with bottom-up initiatives will help to master digital transformation at the Bank and in developing countries.[3] A key role for managerial leadership is to create the security and learning environment for pioneering staff and change agents to operationalize top-down visions and explore new development terrains.

Digital leadership and corporate-wide strategy should also guide research and innovation in digital transformation and scale promising pilots and successful programs. It should aim to move countries from digital disruption to digital transformation. While in the past it was desirable for aid agencies to "wait and see" before adapting to the changing needs of their client countries, today it is an absolute must, if these agencies are to stay relevant and address the growing global challenges facing their clients. Strategies and diagnostic tools can set priorities and allocate resources to various elements of the ecosystem. A strategic decision is to decide who would own or coordinate digital transformation as a whole ecosystem. Will the regional development banks, the UN system, and other aid agencies rise to the challenge, partner with each other, and help countries adapt and thrive in this digital upheaval?

An aid agency strategy should help its staff create the enabling environment for sustainable and inclusive digital transformation in client countries. The Bank's country assistance and partnership strategy should help finance holistic transformation strategies. It should engender client empowerment and ownership. It should build local capacity for digital leadership, institutions, and competencies. It should facilitate learning and innovation at the local level. And given the tendencies of ICT to concentrate power and wealth, development assistance must prioritize the use of ICT and other complementary means to promote economic inclusion.

[3] McNamara used top-down strategy to mainstream urban and rural development programs and used the strategic controls of programming and budgeting and the appointment of senior change agents to implement his vision. JDW tried to do the same with the Strategic Compact and knowledge Bank initiatives.

Staffing and Strategic Resource Allocation

A critical *shortage of staff with up-to-date* digital competencies is the second challenge that aid agencies and their client countries face, especially in the areas of cybersecurity, artificial intelligence, systems integration, change management, digital resilience, digital policy reforms, and digital industry promotion, among others. The IEG found that the Bank has yet to identify the digital skills it needs and to act to fill the gaps. Existing staff with digital skills is insufficient to meet fast-growing client demand. There is a demonstrated need to raise awareness, better leverage existing staff expertise, and share scarce digital skills across different sectors.

Thus far, the Bank's human resource (HR) function has not figured out how to *compete for top digital skills* with high-powered technology corporations. More generally, there are no career streams for technical staff, and little attention to grooming new talent, mentoring, collaboration, and on the job learning—all ingredients for agile learning in a knowledge-based professional organization.

Staff with *hybrid skills in digital application* sectors, such as digital health or digital finance, is also needed to drive transformation in priority sectors. Current career paths at the Bank tend to penalize rather than rewarding hybrid cross-sectoral expertise. Within the digital sector domain, a new breed of staff is needed to promote the health of the national digital transformation ecosystem, beyond the telecom and software development components.

The Bank should encourage two-way *inter-generational learning*. Lacking such incentives often lead to "reinventing the wheel" and losing institutional memory.[4] Inter-generational learning is of particular value when dealing with technological transformation, as younger staff may be up-to-date in technology but often lack experience in the broad institutional, socio-political, and economic contexts of digital transformation. Over the years, I interviewed many Bank staff who were anxious to share their ideas and the challenges they faced with their clients. This is an asset worth mobilizing for development.

[4] This intergenerational knowledge transfer was one of the purposes of the Young Professional Program, but the Program left out the incentives for making this a common practice. Did the Bank's culture promote a YP's belief of becoming an expert in a country or a sector just in a few weeks of joining the institution?

The HR management function in large bureaucracies like the Bank does not always support organizational learning. How can Bank staff keep up with cutting-edge technological advances? How can HR provide incentives for innovation and learning in the context of development? In seeking diversity, for example, the current function tends to ignore *educational and experiential diversity*. The Bank is dominated by economists. Few staff come with relevant private sector experience. Few come from other social sciences and fewer yet with an interdisciplinary background. HR is often neither capable nor empowered by top management to hold managers accountable for creating an adequate environment to help staff pursue inquiry and dialogue and resolve interpersonal and organizational problems arising from addressing new sectors and challenges.

The Bank lacked strategic management *mechanisms to anticipate and reallocate resources* from traditional and/or declining businesses to emerging and promising ones. Strategic allocation of staffing resources demands anticipation of the future needs of stakeholders. For aid agencies, particularly the Bank, the most critical resource to allocate is the operational staff. Most large corporations have processes for portfolio management that redeploy managerial and budgetary resources to promising and innovative businesses of the future. Digital transformation at the Bank is not addressed in this way: traditional sectors continue to monopolize attention and resources. New and cross-cutting dimensions of development tend to have weak internal constituencies.[5] When budgets are tight, competition for resources favors long-established fields. Selectivity often meant shying away from emerging development challenges and focusing on traditional core competencies. Unless staffing and administrative resources are strategically managed, client demand for new emerging dimensions of development will continue to be ignored.

[5] Caveat: traditionally-defined sectors can and need to reinvent themselves to remain relevant and competitive in the allocation process. This sectoral renewal is being accelerated by digital applications in various sectors. With such applications, a transport project today can be significantly different from that of a decade ago.

Culture for Learning, Innovation, and Evaluation

Another learning challenge for large aid bureaucracies is a prevailing institutional *culture that discourages learning, innovation, risk taking, and knowledge sharing*. This is a critical prerequisite to developing competencies for the relatively new and fast-changing field of digital transformation. In such an emerging and cross-cutting field, no one has a final or ready-made solution. Listening to client countries and mobilizing local knowledge and counterparts are often the most important source to learn and innovate. I owe much of my knowledge and learning to my genuine engagement with local stakeholders. This is most likely when the Bank and client country have the incentives and capacity to co-learn.

A cultural barrier to institutional learning is *excessive risk aversion*. Large bureaucracies tend to reward conformity and risk avoidance. Harnessing digital technology for development demands innovation, which is without precedent and inevitably risky. There is no substitute for the process of experimentation and self-discovery. There is no substitute for the process of experimentation and self-discovery. Pretending to have all the answers upfront, rather than learning by doing may have limited the Bank's ability to respond to rapidly changing client needs accelerated by the digital revolution. Despite its perfectionism, the Bank is not infallible. It is easy to take credit for success, and blame failure on country clients. The fear of internal and outside criticism is an obstacle to growth. Risk taking—however informed and calculated—means failing at least some of the time. Clever career-oriented staff often succeed by strangling all risk taking. There is a strong tendency to avoid negative feedback and never question the status quo, to punish risk-takers and discard potentially transformational opportunities.

Prevailing *managerial behaviors and review processes* within the Bank continue to be a major barrier to staff and institutional learning. The entire process management system, starting with proposal reviewers demanding precedents to approve a proposed project, to the types of questions allowed at operational review meetings, all the way to the performance evaluation system do not reward learning from successes and failures, or nurturing creative problem solving and digital innovation.

The Bank's institutional culture is shaped by the *pressure to transfer financial resources* often at the expense of development assistance quality and learning. Success measurement and rewards are tied primarily to the level of lending and the size and number of operations. This lending culture ignores demands for adaptive implementation and continuous learning inherent in the digital transformation ecosystem. Except for emergency assistance situations, Bank learning should be an integral part of Bank lending.

The Bank's intense focus on deliverables and quantitative outputs, while necessary, has led to incentives and performance metrics that do not adequately recognize valuable innovations, institutional learning, and knowledge contributions that are often tacit, long term, and embedded in lending operations. It is important to recognize that most of Bank learning and knowledge is the outcome of listening and working with client governments, civil society, and local entrepreneurs. Acknowledging this requires humility! Operational Bank staff working directly with the clients tend to be more aware of this than the central research department of the Bank. I grew to appreciate this over time, and especially during my field assignments.

The Bank's existing *closed learning model* separates research from operational deliverables and protects the Bank's ideology from internal and external questioning. The Bank's research department prioritizes academic publishing and interaction with the research community over learning from operational experience and interactions with clients. This disconnect may have harmed the digital transformation practice the most.

As currently conceived, the Bank acts as a warehouse of codified knowledge, dogma, and conventional truth. It puts money and prestige behind projects based on implicit assumptions and the claim of superior access to global knowledge. Many of those "truths" imposed by the bureaucratic and financial might of the Bank are likely to be challenged in an open learning environment. If development agencies are to become knowledge-based development assistance institutions, they can no longer pretend to have a monopoly on universally applicable knowledge. Instead, they need to test their assumptions, learn together with their client countries, and adopt a culture of open debate, perhaps from universities and other learning organizations (Ellerman et al. 2001). They would blend local knowledge, tacit knowledge, and social learning with global knowledge, codified knowledge, and centralized learning. The "not invented here" culture, perhaps a product of arrogance, comes at too high a cost.

Learning at aid organizations is generated by connecting field experience and experimentation with research. Learning by doing should be also learning by design. However, operational staff at the Bank is hard-pressed to meet short-term targets and measurable deliverables and is not motivated to integrate research and evaluation findings into those deliverables.

Enabling staff to innovate should be a responsibility of management at all levels. Some aid agencies are considering the creation of a senior manager as chief innovation officer, and building a cadre of innovation officers. Aid agencies may explore various ways to create structures and cultures that promote innovation in development assistance. Innovation is particularly critical to exploring and leveraging digital transformation for development in diverse local contexts.

A culture of learning within aid agencies and in collaboration with client countries would facilitate a better understanding of digital transformation. Countries would lead their own learning and innovation, supported by the agency's global knowledge. Often, aid agencies viewed their clients as passive recipients of the agency's global knowledge.

At the Bank, a significant step to bridge the research-practice gap regarding digital development was the 2016 World Development Report on digital dividends. After decades of ignoring the ongoing digital revolution, this was an encouraging step in addressing the role of digital technologies in development. But that was just one step—much more is needed to operationalize research findings to guide future practice. There must be a strong link between research and operations, economics and other disciplines in order to accelerate organizational learning and capture the complex realities of digital development. Research should also extend to include practical lessons from successful transforming countries that did not get Bank assistance, such as Singapore, Estonia, China, and Taiwan. "Implementation research" is sorely needed.

Over the years I have seen how aid agencies are often hostage to recurrent *fads and ideologies in development economics*. The Bank's Structural Adjustment Lending (SAL), for example, an embodiment of the Washington Consensus and neoliberal ideology in the 1980s and 1990s, persisted for decades with little adaptation despite increasing human costs in Africa, Latin America, and elsewhere. However, SAL has since been replaced by Development Policy Loans (DPL)—applying soft or adaptive conditionalities that should take account of political economy and local implementation capabilities.[6] The financing tool has changed, but that may not guarantee less influence from political and economic

[6] For an early attempt at adapting conditionality and policy learning see "conditionality and policy learning" by Branson and Hanna, in Hanna and Picciotto (2002).

orthodoxy or the skill mix of the staff using the tool to initiate policy reforms.

A former Bank Chief Economist purged research staff who did not conform to the prevailing market fundamentalist ideology at the time. Then, the market fundamentalist majority also argued against addressing the digital revolution for fear of engaging governments in strategic public–private partnerships for managing technological disruption, and perhaps lacking ready answers to the challenges of the digital age.

Ever since the 2008 financial crisis, conventional wisdom about the role of government, financial regulation, and globalization has been questioned. The digital revolution and the rise of the digital economy add more complexity that requires innovation, co-learning, and customized development solutions. It calls for sharing cross-country experiences and developing local capacities to experiment, learn, and address countries' own development priorities.

Ideology can be a powerful enemy of local ownership, learning, and innovation. Neoliberal ideology offers standard solutions to development challenges requiring no local ownership or adaptation. Similarly, it expects ICT to provide standard solutions and requires a homogenized development policy across regions and countries. Experience indicates, however, that authentic development must be locally rooted, which means allowing for diversity of development paths in line with local cultural, historical, and social conditions. Moreover, successful country transformation experience suggests that adoption of new technologies rooted in the local context supports the diversity of development paths in different countries.

A related barrier to organizational learning is weak *systematic and continuous evaluation*, as it applies to the intangible processes of digital transformation. Development practitioners are directed to focus on easily observable and measurable inputs: investment in ICT hardware and software, telecom penetration, Internet connectivity, etc. This creates an incomplete picture of digital development that prevents holistic thinking and learning about intangible components. There is a parallel process of acquiring know-how and capabilities that are difficult to measure, but no less important. These intangible assets are the accumulation of knowledge embedded in people, institutions, and processes. They are key outcomes of systematic learning by doing and continuous and participatory evaluation.

When transformative and innovative projects are designed, the design process generates substantial practical and *tacit knowledge*, but this knowledge is seldom codified and shared. Active "learning by doing" is necessary. Projects and strategies should include monitoring and evaluation designed to generate lessons throughout implementation. Practical knowledge sharing would significantly reduce implementation costs across the portfolio.

In reviewing country transformation cases, I encountered difficulties in accessing reliable information on the *quality of implementation* and independent evaluation of results. Almost all reviews of national digital strategies have been self-reporting exercises, thus lacking independent validation. At the same time many mainstream economists remain skeptical about the transformative impact of digital technology, and its relevance to development policy and practice. Objective evaluation and systematic learning about digital development are squeezed out by these two camps. Using holistic and systematic assessment toolkits for the digital economy, combined with timely independent evaluation, should help. A mind-set of continuous learning and adaptation would also help enhance the effectiveness of WBG support.[7] Most critical is to secure management ownership of evaluation findings—a challenge common among aid agencies.

Country capacity for monitoring, evaluation, and learning should be built from the ground up. It must be holistic and participatory. Holistic digital economy assessment tools are in short supply. Evaluation and learning will require policies and incentives to mobilize demand for good governance and social accountability, including accountability for online services and open data—through enhanced citizen access to information about service delivery and digital dividends. Communities of practice within and across nations should be encouraged to share experience and support along the journey of digital transformation.

Aid agencies' evaluation tools may be contributing to the aversion to innovation, "stretch" targets, and transformational objectives. Many aid projects do not adequately measure development outcomes—confusing

[7] A 2022 IEG (Independent Evaluation Group) study of WBG readiness to "mobilize disruptive and transformation technologies for development" confirmed my own experience. The WBG is implementing an array of Disruptive and Transformative Technologies (DTT) initiatives, yet it is not ready to help clients harness the opportunities and mitigate the growing risks posed by DTTs.

outputs for outcomes. The Bank's own evaluation department's ratings measure a project's success in meeting self-defined targets and objectives but are not meant to assess neither the nature of a project's development outcomes nor the extent to which the project addresses a country's developmental needs. This means these ratings do not account for differing levels of ambition and complexity. High project ratings may also reflect risk aversion through the setting of modest targets and objectives. There are no incentives to operate on the frontier or to risk pursuing higher, transformational development outcomes. Despite rhetoric, aid agencies evaluation tools do not measure or help reward innovation and outcomes.

Partnership Across Sectors and Aid Agencies

Digital transformation demands cross-sectoral collaboration within and among aid agencies, among ministries and other stakeholders within the country, and with local and multinational ICT companies. Digital ecosystems require interoperability, data exchange, and cross-cutting platforms—notions that run against traditional silos or sector-oriented delivery. Mainstreaming digital transformation into development requires partnership among all stakeholders across the entire digital transformation ecosystem. Learning to partner is critical but it is not a common competency of government or aid agencies. A whole-of-government approach to digital transformation of the public sector (and the economy at large) also requires a whole-of-aid agency approach to digital development. Defensiveness of turfs and silos stifles innovation, cooperation and learning.

My 2020 staff interviews as part of the digital economy diagnosis engagement, cited earlier, revealed a lack of collaboration among the Bank's sectoral practices. Competition for task team leadership often led to wasted resources and "reinventing the wheel". Collaboration between the World Bank and the IFC is another matter of concern as successful digital outcomes require knowledge and inputs from both the public and private sectors.

Limited collaboration across the World Bank Group, regional development banks, civil society organizations (CSOs), think tanks, and UN agencies is also a barrier to developmental learning. In my experience, there is much unhealthy competition between the Bank and the regional development banks, despite obvious complementarities and professed desire for collaboration. Many frameworks and assessment tools are developed in isolation or competition: for example, ITU and World Bank on cybersecurity. Similarly, there is mutual suspicion between the Bank and CSOs, although much progress has been made in managing these complex relationships. Specialization should be encouraged but complemented with partnerships to develop and share these tools and standards as global public goods.

CSOs are often better positioned to identify, monitor, and respond to the needs of poor communities. They rely on partnerships and networking, and work across sectors and bureaucratic boundaries. Digital technologies can amplify their voice, connectivity, coordination, and service delivery. They can strengthen resilience and social cohesion. But large organizations like the Bank and government bureaucracies often lack appropriate tools to engage and empower these social intermediaries. New institutional modalities are needed to effectively engage local CSOs with aid agencies in working across sectors and practicing community-driven development. The e-society pilot in e-Sri Lanka program illustrates how small community grants could catalyze partnerships among CSOs and local software houses to leverage digital technologies for local problem solving and inclusive development. The challenge remains for collaboration across development partners to scale up grassroots innovations.

Given the Bank's shortcomings in implementing technical assistance, would it help to complement its financial resource transfer operations with strengthened inputs from other specialized UN agencies? The UN and multilateral development agencies may provide knowledge platforms and nurture communities of practice that cut across all levels of development.[8] UN leadership, however, is struggling to harmonize the increasingly numerous and fragmented digital transformation initiatives across its specialized agencies.

The rhetoric on partnership and multi-stakeholder coordination is not translated into effective collaboration and learning communities.[9] Such collaboration is particularly amiss in the new learning-intensive field of digital transformation where partnership is critical to supporting global digital public goods and minimizing cybersecurity risks. Incentives and

[8] The WBG can provide a learning platform using its Digital Development Partnership (DDP) Fund.

[9] This presumes that specialized UN organizations and other partners are willing to undergo their own digital transformation.

accountability mechanisms need to be reformed to reward collaboration within and across aid agencies.

How about collaborating with multinational and local companies to promote digital transformation and diffusion? While essential, such collaboration requires a balancing act.

On the one hand, there is no denying the critical role of multinational corporations (MNCs) in the diffusion of digital technologies and the build-out of local digital capabilities. Singapore is a great example of how a government can attract MNCs to invest in training and link with nascent local tech companies.

Early on, the World Bank and the IFC engaged in massive privatization and liberalization of the telecom industry. In India and Sri Lanka, local ICT firms and their associations played a central role in developing the digital sector and, more broadly, in helping local public and private sector users pursue digital transformation. ICT-focused FDI helped local companies integrate into global supply chains and create a highly valued ICT export sector.

MNCs promoted best practice sharing, technology transfer, and local innovation. Several companies have contributed to the Digital Development Partnership trust fund—administered by the Bank—to support business development, research, and digital diagnostics tools.

In my personal interaction with Silicon Valley entrepreneurs and consultants at the People-Centered Internet Forum that I had co-founded, I realized that there was immense good will to support innovation that aid agencies could tap for development.

On the other hand, some multinationals engaged in anti-competitive practices leading to telecom monopolies and customers lock-in—thus undermining the local ICT industry. More recently, global technology giants unlawfully used their platforms to capture private data. These monopolistic practices caused excessively high access costs and cognitive dependency, especially in the small and least developed countries in Africa. Excessive dependency of these countries on MNC and aid agency support risks technology determinism while neglecting rising inequality, local adaptation, and sustainability.

Aid agencies must also guard against corruption and conflict of interests. Problems can arise from ICT procurement, given the slow and outdated procurement guidelines of the Bank that are not tailored to the acquisition of software services and new technologies.

In short, global and local tech firms have critical roles to play in digital diffusion. The WBG can act as partner, catalyst, and honest broker. Major aid agencies must build new capabilities to scale up partnerships with the private sector, both locally and globally. I hope that the WBG can act as an honest broker, especially in countries that need it most.

The Bank can aim to be a catalyst and partner for change across all development agencies. In reality, however, despite potential complementarities, there is precious little collaboration between the Bank and regional development Banks.

Most countries are still at the early stages of their digital transformation journeys and have much to learn from each other and from the pioneers. Developed countries have created several regional forums (including the EU) to share knowledge and provide support to policy makers.

Emerging aid donors like India, China, Korea, Singapore, Brazil, and South Africa are pioneering their own South-South partnerships. This is a truly bright spot in digital development. China is investing in telecommunication infrastructure, especially in Africa. India is exploring partnerships for software development in Africa and Sri Lanka. Korea and Singapore are promoting their own digital solutions. Many are learning from Estonia's digital government. It is important to create a platform for sharing lessons learnt, including those I discuss in this book. Aid agencies can also play a catalyzing role in evaluating and sharing these lessons. New actors could expand the menu of strategies and innovations available to active followers. This would help avoid the pitfall of "one-size-fits-all" solutions.

In my long journey through digital development, I experienced first-hand the institutional learning barriers I outlined above. My team and I were seen as "cowboys" and disruptors of the Bank's operating procedures. I celebrated those rare moments of triumph, when we outdid expectations and catalyzed local change. Yet, institutional learning proved at times slow and the barriers frustrating or insurmountable. Diffusion, replicability, and scalability of innovative digital programs across the Bank required the alignment of many institutional factors.

In some country assistance cases, the Bank demonstrated its capacity to learn and cope with the digital revolution. During my engagements in India and Sri Lanka, for example, the Bank managed to overcome multiple barriers thanks to the determination and entrepreneurial spirit of task team leaders, and the client country's commitment to change. Organizational learning was facilitated by a responsive country director, and a personal commitment from the Bank President and the CIO—thus demonstrating that barriers to institutional learning can be overcome when incentives are aligned at all levels of management.

Progress and Challenges

The COVID-19 pandemic has demonstrated to skeptics in the Bank and other aid agencies how critical is digital development to economic and social resilience. At the Bank, it helped transform some long-held practices in management, working across time and space, and delivering services globally. It induced significant change in the "macro" environment for staff engaged in digital development assistance. It accelerated the mainstreaming of digital assistance in bank lending. The Internet extended the reach of participation to engage more policy makers in client countries, consultants, and development partners. More dedicated staff have been assigned to focus on knowledge management and sharing.

With the recent adoption of a more holistic view of digital transformation, an increasing number of countries are able to develop working models and achieve better results. Many countries are now better prepared to partner with the ICT industry and articulate their needs for digital capacity development. There is also more to share through South-South partnerships and open digital platforms. Many countries have become more demanding in their partnerships with the Bank, aid agencies, and MNCs. A higher level of digital maturity of transforming countries has also increased private sector and aid agency confidence in investing in digital technologies. The rise of digital assessment tools has encouraged some countries to view digital transformation in a holistic way and to conduct self-assessments with or without external help.

Digital technologies can help address the multiple crises of the COVID-19 pandemic, climate change, supply chain disruptions, economic inequality, and disparate access to information and responsive public services. While digital technologies can help manage these crises in smart and resilient ways, they also introduce new risks ranging from fintech fraud and destructive uses of artificial intelligence to cyberwars, increased surveillance, human rights abuses, and digital fragility.

How has the Bank responded to these global and country developments?

After some frustratingly slow Bank reactions to the rise of the digital revolution (as demonstrated in earlier chapters), some progress became visible, especially since 2018. Both Jim Kim (former President) and Kristalina Georgieva (former CEO) have signaled a willingness to address the ongoing technological disruptions. The Digital Development Department (DDD) has been elevated to report directly to the global VP for infrastructure. The DDD has since expanded its horizons to include digital ID, public digital platforms, and cybersecurity. Some other global sector practices, such as Governance and Finance, have started to address digital transformation challenges in their respective sectors.

As of May 2023, a dynamic new Bank President has been appointed with extensive business experience and appreciation of the transformative role of digital technologies. Since, the Bank's Executive Directors started discussions with Management on an evolution roadmap covering the Bank's mission, operating model, and financial capacity. The President is expected to create a new VP for digital, who would bring coherence to all elements of the digital transformation ecosystem. In March 2024, he also led a Global Digital Summit to demonstrate Bank commitment to prioritize digital development assistance. These are welcome developments in view of pressing development challenges such as global poverty, inequality, debt burden, climate change, food insecurity, fragility, and conflict, among others. The challenge will be to learn from past experience and move from high aspirations to good practices.

The Bank was able to mobilize significant trust-fund resources from the global ICT industry and bilateral donors to support analytical frameworks, diagnostic tool development, cybersecurity assessments, investment project preparation, and best practice dissemination. Heightened awareness of digital fragility and risks within Bank-funded projects helped increase country demand for digital assistance and Bank responsiveness to such demands.

The digital development partnership (DDP trust fund) enabled different parts of the WBG to coordinate assistance programs for digital payments, digital entrepreneurship, and digital skills. It also helped the Bank to deliver substantial advisory and lending services in Africa. Trust funds also began to support the long-neglected development of assessment tools and frameworks. A notable example is a recently published global study on digital capabilities, which addressed a critical lagging aspect of digital transformation (Melhem and Jacobsen 2022).

The Bank has recently focused on *digital public infrastructure* (DPI), i.e., the underlying network of digital platforms that allow governments to provide vital public services to citizens—from cash transfers and social protection to online education, health, and other public services. DPI includes digital public goods such as open data that can drive forward common global challenges as outlined in the Sustainable Development Goals, from eradicating poverty to gender equality and environmental sustainability.

The COVID-19 pandemic has heightened the importance of an open, accessible, and inclusive DPI for resilience and equality. India was able to vaccinate one billion people within a matter of months thanks to an existing digital vaccination registration system that was facilitated through a public digital infrastructure that brings digital ID and payment platforms together as the "digital roads and bridges" that support the provision of a vast number of digital public services.

What are the challenges ahead?

These recent positive developments are fragile. Deep-seated structural and cultural barriers continue to hinder learning to master digital transformation. Bureaucratic resistance and entrenched cultural norms often defeat the most attractive visions and speedy reorganizations. Experimentation, R&D, and the development of digital assessment frameworks and tools may be episodic and short-lived as they are heavily dependent on trust funds and often viewed as end products rather than as tools to enrich and transform aid practices. At the Bank, incentives and organizational culture remain focused on short-term output and volume of lending. Pressure to finance big projects remains strong, regardless of country preparedness. This often leads to an emphasis on hardware and access to technology, without matching investments in policy and digital capability development and other intangible elements of the digital transformation ecosystem.

The pandemic disruption has not changed the "micro" environment for digital transformation assistance: risk aversion, bureaucratic processes, top-down mandates, excessive safeguards, complex procurement procedures, and rigid implementation practices, among others. These deep-seated cultural and structural changes are critical to translate corporate policies and commitments into tools, standards, skills, incentives, partnerships, and adaptive implementation. Diagnostic tools, by themselves, do not guarantee diversity of thought, avoid conformity, empower clients, or secure a powerful learning environment.

Challenges must be acknowledged to enable faster and deeper learning. Digital transformation across the WBG portfolio remains weak. Some main elements of the digital transformation ecosystem are lagging or fragmented across user sectors such as digital health, education, governance, and environment. Rivalries among sectoral practices within the Bank and among aid agencies have led to the proliferation and duplication of digital assessment tools causing waste and costly assessment fatigue among less prepared clients.

Current assessment tools tend to neglect the digital divide and the needs of the poor. Driven by the ever-increasing pressure to lend, the Bank and other financing agencies continue to sacrifice project quality, innovation, and institution building. This pressure is compounded by the emerging sovereign debt crisis in many low- and middle-income countries. While debt stress has impact on all development sectors, digital transformation of public finance can help countries to rationalize and optimize public expenditure, improve debt management, increase transparency, and improve tax collection.

An ambitious reform agenda would take advantage of the digital revolution to realize a truly innovative, knowledge-based, and smart solutions Bank. It would harness the digital revolution to address the interdependent global challenges of climate change, pandemics, food insecurity, and governance. These global crises should be viewed as opportunities to build, reform and transform global organizations, and leverage digital technologies for development.

Country digital strategies should be driven by and aligned with overall country development strategies. Digital transformation offers powerful means that can be tailored to the specific needs and conditions of each developing country, and their own set of Sustainable Development Goals (SDGs).[10]

While the Bank and other aid agencies are beginning to appreciate the growing digital infrastructure risks, they are still oblivious of the need to address the broader societal risks such as rising inequality. The shortfall in digital risk management capabilities stands in stark contrast to rising risk demands. Similarly, while digital diagnostic tools can stimulate the desire to advance in country rankings, they may reinforce dependency

[10] An alarming recent trend is the slowing progress, and in some cases the reversal of progress to achieve the SDGs in many developing countries. By UN count, of the 140 metrics for achieving these goals, half are not on the desired trajectory and about one-third have stalled or gone into reverse. About 60% of low-income countries face debt distress. There is no room for complacency.

on external technical assistance, unless used specifically for empowerment and capacity building. Yet, incentives to use these tools to empower clients and build local capacity remain weak.

The disruptive impact of digital technology on jobs and inequality is likely to increase. Artificial intelligence (AI) is the latest wave of technologies to promise a leap in digital transformation. This calls upon all development stakeholders, including government, private sector, civil society, and citizens to engage and govern such new and critical technologies. New partnerships and institutions are needed to manage this digital transition, and moderate the strategic risks. Sustaining the march toward digital transformation will require much innovation in policies and investments to secure inclusive development.

Shaping the Future

In conclusion, there is still much work to do for aid agencies and development partners to acknowledge and overcome past mistakes and to bring development practices in sync with the pace of the digital revolution. There is a real risk that growing demands placed on the Bank and other aid agencies would divert attention from the necessary reforms to master digital transformation. In fact, they offer a rare window of opportunity to prepare for the future by treating digital transformation as a foundation or enabler to implement the growing development agenda. It is a major opportunity to build smart economies and practice development 2.0. The future is digital.

It is important to recognize that while the institutional learning barriers I described are critical, they are neither immutable nor insurmountable. These learning barriers should be taken seriously. The diffusion and mainstreaming of digital transformation within the Bank are slow, mainly due to institutional learning constraints. While such constraints are common across sectors and aid agencies, they tend to slow the pace of developmental learning and innovation at a time when the digital revolution and global development challenges are most pressing.[11] The digital revolution is fast-paced and pervasive, and its outcomes are

[11] Some observers of Bank effectiveness (such as Nick Stern, former chief economist of the Bank) might argue that the Bank's contribution to development thinking looks relatively weak when the Bank is rated as an innovator but looks quite strong as a screener, adopter, and diffuser (of thought and practice) of innovation.

contingent on many contextual and complementary factors. It intensifies the learning and risk management requirements for countries and aid agencies. The premium for rapid response and agile learning in the digital age is at an all-time high. Aid agencies could and should do better in the future.

What will the future look like? Our future will not be decided by data, Internet, or artificial intelligence alone. Transformative technologies defy predictions. Hopefully, the future will be shaped by shared human values, culture, and creativity as digital technologies transform economies and relationships among government, business, civil society, and citizens. Developing countries need to imagine and anticipate their future to identify opportunities arising from the digital revolution. We need to rehearse the future to understand the opportunities, risks, and uncertainties ahead.

Mastering digital transformation at global aid organizations and developing countries calls for a new style of leadership that is central to profound, sustained, transformational change. At aid agencies, this means leadership that is open, collaborative, and vision-driven. Managers must empower staff to learn, innovate, and serve clients. They must set free the substantial talent and creativity of their staff to co-create with client country leaders, and empower ecosystem stakeholders. The digital revolution opens a window of opportunity for practicing this style of leadership that nurtures innovation and leverages new technologies to alleviate poverty and power sustainable development.

I remain optimistic. I have a dream. I dream of development practice in the digital age as it should be and ask: why not?

My Relevant Publications

Ellerman, D., S. Denning, and Nagy K. Hanna. 2001. "'Active Learning and Development Assistance' in 'Tacit Knowledge Exchange and Active Learning'." Special issue: *Journal of Knowledge Management* 5 (2): 171–179.

Nagy K. Hanna. 1985. *Strategic Planning and Management*. World Bank Discussion Paper. Washington, DC: World Bank. https://documents.worldbank.org/en/publication/documents-reports/documentdetail/562811468765919659/strategic-planning-and-management-a-review-of-recent-experience

———. 1990. *Development in the Information Age: An Evolving Role for the World Bank*. World Bank, Mimeo.

———. 1991. *The Information Technology Revolution and Economic Development*. World Bank Discussion Paper 120. Washington, DC: World Bank. https://elibrary.worldbank.org/doi/abs/10.1596/0-8213-1784-9

———.2007a. *From Envisioning to Designing e-Development: The Experience of Sri Lanka*. Washington, DC: World Bank. http://documents.worldbank.org/curated/en/438421468104642480/From-envisioning-to-designing-e-development-the-experience-of-Sri-Lanka

———. 2007b. *e-Leadership Institutions for the Knowledge Economy*. Washington, DC: World Bank.

———. 2008. *Transforming Government and Empowering Communities: The Sri Lanka Experience*. Directions in Development Series. Washington, DC: World Bank. https://openknowledge.worldbank.org/handle/10986/6345?locale-attribute=en

———. 2009. *e-Transformation: Enabling New Development Strategies*. New York: Springer.

N. K. Hanna, *Economic Development in the Digital Age*,
https://doi.org/10.1007/978-3-031-54569-6

———. 2010. *Transforming Government and Building the Information Society*. New York: Springer.

———. 2011. *Enabling Enterprise Transformation: Business and Grassroots Innovation for the Knowledge Economy*. New York: Springer.

———. 2012a. *Open, Smart, and Inclusive Development: ICT for Transforming North Africa*. Abidjan: African Development Bank.

———. 2012b. *Transforming to a Networked Society: Guide for Policy Makers*. Gaithersburg, MD: Sriban, 2015.

———. 2016a. *Mastering Digital Transformation*. Bingley: Emerald.

———. 2016b. "e-Commerce as a Techno-Managerial Innovation Ecosystem: Policy Implications." *Journal of Innovation Management* 4 (1): 4–10.

———. 2016c. "Thinking About Digital Dividends." *Information Technology & International Development* 12 (3): 25–30. A review and critique of the WBR2016: *Digital Dividends*.

———. 2017. *How Can Digital Technologies Improve Public Services and Governance?* New York, NY: Business Expert Press.

———. 2018. "Role of the State in the Digital Age." *Journal of Innovation and Entrepreneurship* 7: 5. https://doi.org/10.1186/s13731-018-0086-3.

———.. 2020. "Assessing the Digital Economy." *Journal of Innovation and Entrepreneurship* 9: 16. https://doi.org/10.1186/s13731-020-00129-1

Nagy K. Hanna, and Sandor Boyson. 1993. *Information Technology in World Bank lending: Increasing the Developmental Impact*. World Bank Discussion Paper. Washington, DC: World Bank.

Nagy K. Hanna, and Peter Knight. 2011a. *Seeking Transformation Through Information Technology: Strategies for Brazil, China, Canada and Sri Lanka*. New York: Springer.

———. 2011b. *National Strategies to Harness Information Technology: Seeking Transformation in Singapore, Finland, the Philippines, and South Africa*. New York: Springer.

Nagy K. Hanna, and Robert Picciotto (co-authors and co-editors). 2002. *Making Development Work*. Transaction Publishers. New Jersey.

Nagy K. Hanna, and Robert Picciotto, eds. 2002. *Making Development Work*. New Brunswick, NJ: Transaction Publishers.

Nagy K. Hanna, and C. Qiang. 2009. Trends in National e-Government Institutions. In *Information and Communications for Development 2009: Extending Reach and Increasing Impact*. Washington, DC: The World Bank.

———. 2010. China's Informatization Strategy. In *International Experience in e-Development*. Washington, DC: World Bank.

Nagy K. Hanna, Guy, and E. Arnold. 1995. *The Diffusion of Information Technology: Experience of Industrial Countries and Lessons for Developing Countries*. World Bank Discussion Paper. Washington, DC: World Bank.

Nagy K. Hanna, S. Boyson, and S. Gunaratne. 1996. *The East Asian Miracle and Information Technology: Strategic Management of Technological Learning*. World Bank Discussion Paper. Washington, DC: World Bank.

Nagy K. Hanna, et al. 2000. *1999 Annual Review of Development Effectiveness*. World Bank Operations Evaluation Department. Washington, DC: World Bank.

References

Acemoglu, Daron, and James A. Robinson. 2012. "Why Nations Fail: The Origins of Power, Prosperity, and Poverty." *ASEAN Economic Bulletin* 29: 168.

———. 2013. "Economics Versus Politics: Pitfalls of Policy Advice." Journal of Economic Perspectives 27 (2): 173–192.

Acemoglu, Daron, Aghion Philippe, and Fabrizio Zilibotti. 2002. "Distance to Frontier, Selection, and Economic Growth." National Bureau of Economic Research, July.

Amsden, Alice. 1989. *Asia's Next Giant: South Korea and Late Industrialization*. New York: Oxford University Press.

Argyris, Chris, and Donald Schon. 1974. *Theory in Practice: Increasing Professional Effectiveness.* San Francisco: Jossey-Bass.

Asian Development Bank. 2022. *CAREC Digital Strategy 2030: Accelerating Digital Transformation for Regional Competitiveness and Inclusive Growth.* Manila: ADB.

Ayres, R.U. 1989. "Technological Transformation and Long Waves." Research Report 98-1. International Institute for Applied Systems Analysis.

Brynjolfsson, E., and A. Saunders. 2010. *Wired for Innovation: How Information Technology Is Reshaping the Economy*. Boston, MA: MIT Press.

Brynjolfsson, E., and A. McAfee. 2017. *Machine, Platform, Crowd*. New York, NY: Norton.

Carr, Nicholas. 2004. *Does It Matter? Information Technology and the Corrosion of Competitive Advantage*. Boston: Harvard Business School Press.

Commission on Growth and Development. 2008. *The Growth Report: Strategies for Sustained Growth and Inclusive Development*. Washington, DC: World Bank.

Dahlman, Routti, and Yla-Anttila. 2006. *Finland as a Knowledge Economy*. Washington, DC: World Bank.

Davies, Richard. 2019. *Extreme Economies*. London: Bantam Press.

Dercon, Stefan. 2022. *Gambling on Development: Why Some Countries Win and Others Lose*. London: Hurst and Company.

Easterly, William. 2007. *The White Man's Burden: Why the West's Efforts to Aid the Rest Have Done So Much Ill and So Little Good*. New York: Oxford University Press.

———. 2015. *The Tyranny of Experts: Economists, Dictators, and the Forgotten Rights of the Poor*. New York, NY: Basic Books.

Ellerman, David. 2002. "Helping People Help Themselves: Autonomy-Compatible Assistance." In *Making Development Work*, edited by N. Hanna and R. Picciotto. New Brunswick, NJ: Transaction Publishers.

Evans, Peter. 1995. *Embedded Autonomy: States and Industrial Transformation*. Princeton, NJ: Princeton University Press.

Goldman, M., H. Ergas, E. Ralf, and G. Felker. 2013. *Technology Institutions and Policies*. Washington, DC: World Bank.

Gurin, J. 2013. *Open Data Now*. New York: McGraw-Hill Education.

Harari, Yuval. 2019. *21 Lessons for the 21st Century*. New York: Spiegel & Grau.

Hirschman, Albert O. 1958. *The Strategy for Economic Development*. New Haven: Yale University Press.

———. 1967 and 2002. *Development Projects Observed*. Washington, DC: Brookings Institution.

ITU. 2010. "National e-Strategies for Development: Global Status and Prospects, 2010."

Karnik, Kiran. 2012. *The Coalition of Competitors*. New Delhi: Collins Business.

Katz, Raul, and Fernando Callorda. 2018. *The Economic Contribution of Broadband, Digitization, and ICT Regulation*. Geneva: International Telecommunications Union.

———. 2020. *The Economic Contribution of Broadband, Digitization, and ICT Regulation: Econometric Modelling for Arab States*. Geneva: International Telecommunications Union.

Kaufmann, Daniel. 2002. *Rethinking Governance*. Washington, DC: World Bank Institute, World Bank, December.

Khanna, Ro. 2023. *Progressive Capitalism*. New York, NY: Simon & Schuster.

Komninos, N. 2008. *Intelligent Cities and Globalization of Innovation Networks*. London: Routledge.

Lall, Sanjay. 2004. "Reinvesting Industrial Strategy: The Role of Government Policy in Building Industrial Competitiveness." G-24 Discussion Paper No. 28. Geneva: United Nations, April.

Mehta, Harish. 2022. *The Inside Story of a Movement That Shaped India's IT Revolution*. Gurugram: Harper Business India.

Melhem, Samia, and Astrid Herdis Jacobsen. 2022. *A Global Study on Digital Capabilities*. Washington, DC: World Bank Group.

Ndulu, Benno, Elizabeth Stuart, Stefan Dercon, and Peter Knaack. 2023. *Driving Digital Transformation: Lessons from Seven Developing Countries*. New York: Oxford University Press.

Nelson, Richard R. 2004. "The Changing Institutional Requirements for Technological Catch Up." Columbia University, June.

North, Douglass C. 1990. *Institutions, Institutional Change and Economic Performance*. New York: Cambridge University Press.

Perez, Carlota. 2002. *Technological Revolutions and Financial Capital*. Cheltenham: Edward Elgar.

Rodrik, Dani. 2007. *One Economics, Many Recipes*. Princeton: Princeton University.

Sabel, Charles F., and Sanjay Reddy. n.d. "Learning to Learn: Undoing the Gordian Knot of Development Today." Colombia University.

Sachs, Jeffrey. 2014. *The Age of Sustainable Development*. New York: Columbia University Press.

Saxenian, Anna Lee. 2002. *The New Argonauts: How Entrepreneurs Are Linking Technology Markets in a Global Economy*. Cambridge: Harvard University Press.

Schmidt, Eric, and Jared Cohen. 2014. *The New Digital Age*. New York: Vintage Books.

Sen, Amartya. 2000. *Development as Freedom*. New York: Anchor Books Edition.

Southwood, R. 2022. *Africa 2.0: Inside a Continent's Communications Revolution*. Manchester: Manchester University Press.

Spence, Michael. 2011. *The Next Convergence*. New York: Farrar, Straus and Giroux.

Stiglitz, Joseph, and Bruce Greenwold. 2014. *Creating a Learning Society*. New York: Columbia University Press.

Tapscott, Don. 1997. *The Digital Economy: Promise and Peril in the Age of Networked Intelligence*. New York: McGraw-Hill.

Tapscott, Don, and Anthony D. Williams. 2010. *Macrowikinomics: Rebooting Business and the World*. New York: Penguin Group.

Townsend, Anthony M. 2013. *Smart Cities*. New York: W. W. Norton.

UNCTAD. 2013. *The Information Economy Report 2013: The Cloud Economy and Developing Countries*. New York: UN.

———. 2016. "Issues Paper on Foresight for Digital Development." UNCTAD.

———. 2019. *Digital Economy Report 2019: Value Creation and Capture: Implications for Developing Countries*. New York: UN. https://doi.org/10.18356/c7dc937a-en.

United Nations (UN). "e-Government Surveys: 2010, 2012, 2014, 2016, 2018." http://unpan1.un.org/intradoc/groups/public/documents/un/unpan047965.pdf

Unwin, T. 2017. *Reclaiming Information & Communication Technologies for Development*. Oxford University Press.

Wade, Robert. 1990. *Governing the Market*. Princeton, NJ: Princeton University Press.

World Bank. 1993. *The East Asia Miracle: Economic Growth and Public Policies*. New York: Oxford University Press.

———. 1998. *Beyond the Washington Consensus: Institutions Matter*. Washington, DC: World Bank.

———. 1999. *Knowledge for Development, World Development Report 1998–99*. Washington, DC: World Bank.

———. 2009. *Information and Communications for Development 2009. Extending Reach and Increasing Impact*. Washington, DC: World Bank.

———. 2012a. *ICT for Greater Development Impact: World Bank Group Strategy for Information and Communication Technology*. Washington, DC: World Bank.

———. 2012b. *Maximizing Mobile*. Washington, DC: World Bank.

———. 2014. "Independent Evaluation Group. Implementation Completion and Results Report for e-Sri Lanka Project." Washington, DC: World Bank, September 17.

———. 2016. *Digital Dividends*. World Development Report. Washington, DC: World Bank.

——— (Kelly, Tim, Aleksandra Liaplina, Shawn W. Tan, and Hernan Winkler). 2017. *Reaping Digital Dividends: Leveraging the Internet for Development in Europe and Central Asia. Europe and Central Asia Studies*. Washington, DC: World Bank.

———. 2018a. *Competing in the Digital Age: Policy Implications for the Russian Federation*. Washington, DC: World Bank.

———. 2018b. *Malaysia's Digital Economy: A New Driver for Development*. Washington, DC: World Bank.

———. 2019a. *Nigeria Digital Economy Diagnostic Report*. Washington, DC: World Bank.

———. 2019b. *Data-Driven Development*. Washington DC: World Bank.

———. 2021. *Mobilizing Technology for Development: An Assessment of World Bank Group Preparedness*. Independent Evaluation Group. Washington, DC: World Bank.

——— (Cruz, Marcio, Mark A. Dutz, and Carlos Rodríguez-Castelán). 2022a. *Digital Senegal for Inclusive Growth: Technological Transformation for Better and More Jobs*. Washington, DC: World Bank.

———. 2022b. *South Asia's Digital Opportunity: Accelerating Growth, Transforming Lives*. Washington, DC: World Bank.

———. 2024. Digital Progress and Trends Report 2023. Washington, DC: World Bank.

World Bank. Internal Audit Department (IAD). 1998. *Report on Follow Up Review of Informatics*. Washington, DC: World Bank.

World Economic Forum. 2012. "Big Data, Big Impact: New Possibilities for International Development." World Economic Forum.
———. 2015. "The Global Information Technology Report 2015." World Economic Forum.

Index

N. K. Hanna, *Economic Development in the Digital Age*, https://doi.org/10.1007/978-3-031-54569-6

The manufacturer's authorised representative in the EU is Springer Nature Customer Service Centre GmbH, Europaplatz 3, 69115 Heidelberg, Germany. If you have any concerns regarding our products, please contact ProductSafety@springernature.com

Printed and bound by CPI Group (UK) Ltd, Croydon, CR0 4YY
01/10/2026
02225879-0015